This book is dedicated to my late partner, Lee Bailey Norris, with whom I shared many skiing, kayaking, and birdwatching adventures. Lee, "a falcon, tow'ring in her pride of place, Was by a mousing owl hawk'd at, and killed." (*Macbeth*, 2.4.12)

# Cross-Country
# skiing
# California

### Groomed Trails
### and
### Where to Stay
### From Mount Shasta to Kings Canyon

## Michael Jeneid

WILDERNESS PRESS
BERKELEY

First Edition January 2000

Copyright © 1999 by Michael Jeneid
Photographs by the author except where noted
Map © 1999 by Jaan Hitt

Book design by Jaan Hitt
Cover design by Jaan Hitt
Front cover photo: © 1993 by Kevin Lahey/Shasta Ski Park
Back cover photo: © 2000 by David Madison/Royal Gorge
Spine photo: © 2000 by David Madison/Royal Gorge

Library of Congress Card Catalog Number 99-056083
ISBN 0-89997-246-2

Manufactured in the United States of America

Published by **Wilderness Press**
**1200 5th Street**
**Berkeley, CA 94710**
**(800) 443-7227; FAX (510) 558-1696**
*mail@wildernesspress.com*

Contact us for a free catalog
Visit our web site at www.wildernesspress.com

Printed on recycled paper, 20% post-consumer waste

**Library of Congress Cataloging-in-Publication Data**
Jeneid, Michael.
    Cross-country skiing in California:groomed trails and where to stay from
    Mount Shasta to Kings Canyon/ Michael Jeneid.--1st ed.
        p. cm.
    Includes bibliographical references and index.
    ISBN 0-89997-246-2 (alk. paper)
        1. Cross-country skiing--California--Guidebooks. 2. Cross-country skiing
--Tahoe, Lake, Region (Calif. and Nev.)--Guidebooks. 3. Cross-country ski trails--
California--Guidebooks. 4. Cross-country ski trails--Tahoe, Lake, Region (Calif. and
Nev.)--Guidebooks. 5. California--Guidebooks. 6. Tahoe, Lake, Region (Calif. and
Nev.)--Guidebooks. I. Title.

GV855.5. C2 J46 2000

                    99-056083

Frontis photo: © 2000 David Madison/Royal Gorge

| Area | | Lowest Elevation | Groomed Trail (km) | With Own Lodging | Telemark Lifts | On-site Rentals | Ski School | Dogs Allowed | Snowshoeing | Special Features |
|---|---|---|---|---|---|---|---|---|---|---|
| 1 | Shasta Ski Park | 5,245' | 31 | - | 4 | yes | yes | yes | yes | cs |
| 2 | Eagle Mountain | 5,732' | 86 | - | - | yes | yes | - | yes | - |
| 3 | Royal Gorge | 6,700' | 328 | yes | 4 | yes | yes | yes | yes | cs/gp/sm |
| 4 | Royal Gorge Wilderness Lodge | 6,700' | 328 | yes | 4 | yes | yes | - | yes | sr/gm/gp |
| 5 | Clair Tappaan Lodge | 7,000' | 12 | yes | - | yes | yes | - | yes | - |
| 6 | ASI—Donner Spitz Hutte | 7,200' | - | yes | yes | - | yes | - | yes | ms |
| 7 | Auburn Ski Club | 7,100' | 15 | - | yes | - | yes | - | - | sj/b/tc |
| 8 | Tahoe Donner | 6,500' | 100 | - | yes | yes | yes | - | yes | cs |
| 9 | Resort at Squaw Creek Olympic Valley | 6,000' | 18 | yes | yes | yes | yes | - | yes | s/is/sr |
| 10 | Tahoe Cross Country | 6,300' | 65 | - | - | yes | yes | - | yes | gsr |
| 11 | North Tahoe Regional Park | 6,232' | 10 | - | - | - | - | yes | yes | lc |
| 12 | northstar-at-tahoe™ | 6,600' | 65 | yes | yes | yes | yes | - | yes | tl |
| 13 | Diamond Peak | 8,200' | 40 | - | - | yes | yes | yes | yes | |
| 14 | Spooner Lake | 7,000' | 65 | yes | - | yes | yes | - | yes | gp |
| 15 | Camp Richardson Resort | 6,240' | 35 | yes | - | yes | - | - | yes | sr/gm |
| 16 | Sorensen's | 7,000' | - | yes | - | yes | yes | yes | yes | d |
| 17 | Caples Lake Resort | 7,800' | - | yes | - | yes | - | - | yes | gm |
| 18 | Kirkwood Cross Country | 7,800' | 80 | yes | yes | yes | yes | yes | yes | gp |
| 19 | Bear Valley Cross Country | 7,000' | 65 | yes | yes | yes | yes | - | yes | cs |
| 20 | Yosemite Cross Country Ski Center | 6,500' | 17 | yes | yes | yes | yes | - | yes | - |
| 21 | Tamarack Lodge Resort | 8,600' | 40 | yes | - | yes | yes | ot | ot | gm |
| 22 | Montecito Sequoia | 6,600' | 60 | yes | 1 | yes | yes | - | yes | is |

**Abbreviations**

b-biathlon rifle range
cs-child ski school
d-dogsled
gm-great meal
gp-great packages

gsr-great ski race (March)
is-ice skating
lc-low cost
ms-mountaineering skills clinics
ot-off-trail
s-swimming

sj-(nordic) ski jump
sm-snow making
sr-sleigh ride
tc-(membership-based) training center
tl-telemark lessons

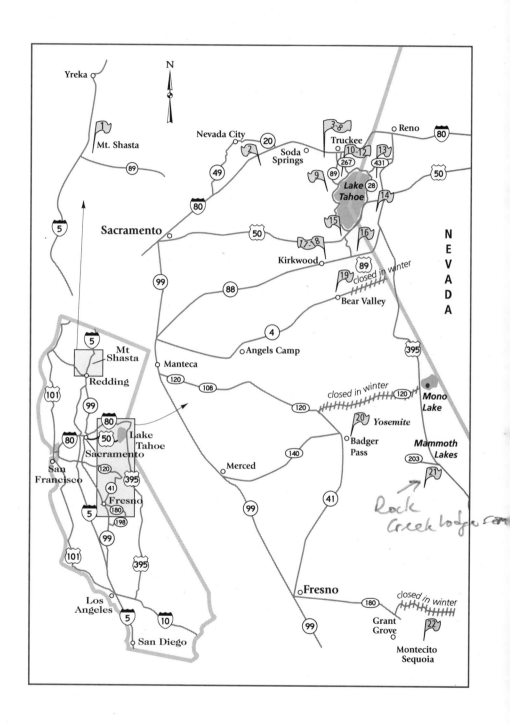

N

Yreka

Mt. Shasta

Nevada City

Soda Springs

3-8

Truckee

Reno

80

10-12

267

13

431

49

20

2

9

89

Lake Tahoe

28

14

50

80

Sacramento

50

16

17-18

N E V A D A

Kirkwood

89

closed in winter

19

99

88

Bear Valley

4

Angels Camp

395

5

Mt Shasta

Redding

Manteca

101

99

120

108

closed in winter

120

Mono Lake

80

50

Lake Tahoe

Sacramento

San Francisco

120

395

41

Fresno

5

180

198

120

20

Yosemite

Badger Pass

203

Mammoth Lakes

140

Merced

21

99

41

Rock Creek lodges on

99

101

395

Los Angeles

5

10

Fresno

180

closed in winter

San Diego

99

Grant Grove

22

Montecito Sequoia

# *"Langlaufers* Live Longer"

This was the title of a magazine article about cross-country skiing that I read while recovering from phlebitis in both legs, pneumonia, and a pulmonary embolism—the result of a rather harsh voyage at sea. I had been 12 days in an open whale boat in freezing weather, bringing it down from Hurricane Island in Maine to Manhattan's 79th Street Yacht Basin. I was soon to be released from the George Washington Hospital. While regaining strength my doctor had warned me, "Michael, you must take it easier for a couple of years; you've been set back a bit." I was 38 years old.

On reading the article, my relief was palpable. I knew that *langlauf* was the German word for cross-country skiing. According to *"Langlaufers* Live Longer," the optimal use of all limbs and muscles combined with cardiovascular effort—while striding and gliding on skis—is the best overall exercise known to the medical profession. "That's for me," I thought, and asked my doctor for his opinion the next day. "Excellent," he said. "Go ahead—do it!"

I didn't know how to ski. I didn't know that Alpine skiing and Cross-country (also known as Nordic) skiing were two separate sports. Since my wife was an experienced Alpine skier, she encouraged me to borrow her skis and a friend's boots; off I went to the Central Park slopes. There was plenty of snow in the park, and the children sledding were having a wonderful time. Yet later, with blisters on my heels, I was wondering why skiing, which looked easy, was so difficult. Obviously, I needed lessons.

My wife and I went to Killington in Vermont for a skiing vacation, where a full week's instruction in Alpine skiing proved enjoyable but expensive. I saw some cross-country skiers having a good time there without using the lifts. A free heel on lightweight skis for walking and gliding wherever—up- and downhill—appealed to me. I decided that cross-country was for me.

At Phoenix House Programs, the NYC residential facility for convicted drug addicts, I introduced cross-country skiing to the Outward Bound-style adventure program I directed. After my illness, it was an opportunity to share what the founder of Outward Bound, Dr. Kurt Hahn, had written of his own life experience: "Let your debility become your opportunity."

Cross-country skiing rapidly became my way of life. I left the hospital in January 1969, and by March the following year I was one of the nearly 10,000 men (women were barred at that time) assembled before dawn on the snow flats beside the Dalaven River in Sweden. We were there to ski the *Vasalopp*—an incredible 53.6 miles from Salen to Mora across Dalarna Province—to be done in one day. After racing with limited visibility and falling snow, the winner completed the course in 5 hours, 35 minutes, and it took me almost 10. But I finished*. After skiing that race five times, my time was down to 6 hours, 7 minutes, and I won a coveted *Vasa* medal.

In 1972, I was fully certified as a Nordic ski instructor by the Professional Ski Instructors of America, and I became head of the Outdoor

*The 50-km Gold Rush at Royal Gorge that caps the national series of races known as The Great American Ski Chase*

Adventure Department at Boston University. With my students I explored Vermont's Green Mountains on skis while living in the clean white snow. Many of the students took up non-competitive cross-country skiing as their primary winter recreation, some shared my own quest to become an expert skier and racer.

In 1975 I left the university to become a full-time, marathon ski racer, starting a ski school to support my new lifestyle. Racing took me to all the great championships in Norway, Finland, Sweden, Italy, Germany, Austria, and Switzerland. Yet, Canada's 100-mile *Coureurs de Bois*, from Lachute in Quebec to Hull in Ontario, is the greatest cross-country ski race of all. Capping the rugged winding course through the Laurentian Mountains is a wonderful dinner and award ceremony in Hull's huge armory.

In Hull I had the great privilege of holding a door open for Jack Rabbit Johansen. A Swedish engineer and lifetime cross-country skier, Jack Rabbit had designed many of Canada's ski areas. He was the guest of honor and principal speaker after my second *Coureurs de Bois*. He spoke about the value of cross-country skiing for mental and physical health; the character building it develops; and its pleasure. He spoke to 2,000 skiers fluently for five minutes in each of four languages: English, French, German, and Swedish. Thunderous was the applause after each language phase, but when he stepped down I thought the great hall's rafters might come down. He was tall and slender and unbowed. When I opened a door for him after the speech he turned and said, "You have no need to hold the door." So I replied, "I know, sir, but it gives me great pleasure to do it." And he smiled. Jack Rabbit was 104 years old when he made that speech, and he was still skiing 5 kilometers every day.

≈

In 1978 I came to California to start a Nordic ski school at the Sierra Club's Clair Tappaan Lodge, close to Sugar Bowl and Donner Ski Ranch. While ours was a small in-house operation, our neighbor John Slouber at Royal Gorge was developing the largest cross-country ski resort in North America. In the next eight years, besides running the Sierra Club school, I wrote a guide to help skiers turn and stop without falling**. After a season at Royal Gorge I moved to the Bay Area to write full-time. In 1999 I'm back on California's finest groomed trails, researching and writing a guide to help new skiers get started and encourage old-timers to explore new areas.

From the resorts of Mt. Shasta south to Lake Tahoe and farther south to those of Kirkwood, Bear Mountain, Yosemite, Mammoth Mountain, and Kings Canyon, I've skied all 22 areas covered in this book this year. In the following pages excellent hotels, rustic lodges, and good food are described. I offer this encouragement in the language of Jack Rabbit Johansen for all who ski the Nordic way: *Heja, heja, friskt humor, det er det som susan jore!* (Go on, go on, have the spirit; it's what will get you there!)

*I chronicled my physical and spiritual preparation for this event in a journal entitled, *The Way to Mora*, published by Walking News in New York.

**My illustrated guide, published by The Nordic Press, is called *Five Easy Turns* and provides the basis for much of Chapter 3.

## Note to Readers

For cross-country ski areas that didn't have their '99-'00 prices available in time for publication, last season's prices are quoted. Prices are usually raised a small amount each season (and in a few instances there are slight reductions). To verify current prices, check the Web sites listed for most areas or give them a call. One ski area, formerly Lakeview at Tahoe City, now called Tahoe Cross Country, has changed the names of all its trails from local wildlife to colors (from the colors of ski waxes). Their new trail map shows this. Because every ski area provides you with their own detailed yet easy-to-follow trail map when you purchase your pass, trail maps aren't included in this book.

Mountain Adventure Seminars—Basecamp Lodge, (209) 753-6556, has purchased Red Dog Lodge at Bear Valley as its new headquarters. It offers dormitory accommodations and breakfast for $25. Their program includes use of Bear Valley Cross Country's groomed trails, but their emphasis is on telemark and wilderness skiing.

# Acknowledgments

My thanks to the ski-resort operators and hotel owners and managers who went out of their way to assist me as I traveled throughout the winter of '98-'99, skiing all the areas in this book. John Slouber (Royal Gorge), Max Jones (Spooner Lake), and Paul Petersen (Bear Valley) were especially generous with their time and facilities. Without your help there would have been no book. A special note of commendation to the groomers who work at night setting up the next day's skiing. Thanks to Keatin Holly for reading the manuscript and giving a freshman skier's feedback. Thanks to all the photographers whose credited images are everywhere in the book. High praise and thanks to Daphne Hougard without whose action photography there would be no exercise and turning-on-skis sections in the book. Thanks to Tim Larive of Shasta Ski Park and photographer Kevin Lahey for providing the book's cover shot. My telemark skis and backcountry boots were provided by the Fischer and Salomon reps in Truckee and prepared for me by Paco's Bike and Ski Shop. Finally, my thanks to my editor, Paul Backhurst, whose pluming skills have always been matched by his enthusiasm for the project.

—Michael Jeneid

# 1   A Survey of Nordic Skiing
# —in Europe and the US

## National Contributions

Nordic skiing, also known as cross-country skiing in the United States, is the traditional name for the national sport of Norway, Sweden, and Finland. Those of us who use the "Nordic" term do so because we appreciate the home origins of the sport. Anyone who watched on television will remember the Winter Olympics of 1996 at Lillehammer in Norway. In these games a Norwegian cross-country superstar, Bjorn Dahli, became the winner of the most medals in the history of the Olympics. After three games his total was ten medals, one more than Carl Lewis's. Dahli had the panache to collect one of his gold medals at Lillehammer while crossing the finish line—skiing backwards.

These three Nordic countries have the longest history of people skiing to work and to play. While horses, dogs, reindeer, and snowmobiles can be used to tow a skier over snow in a method of conveyance called skijoring, being pulled has no part in real skiing because it aborts the intrinsic reward of being self-propelled. Even today, one of the joys of living in snowbound Nordica is to see kids from eight to 18 years old skiing to school. Many ski several miles each morning and when they reach town they climb up onto the berm, made by snow that's been cleared from the road, and ski on that all the way to their classroom.

By adding Denmark to this Nordic triad you gain a nation more famous for badminton than skiing, but the Danes do ski cross-country even though they don't get much snow. They take their skiing holidays farther north, going as far as Greenland where they find the best skiers for their Danish

Nordic team. Many years ago when I raced in Norway against this team, their slowest skier was the only Dane among them. The rest were very good, and I discovered they were all ringers from Greenland.

The French enjoy Nordic skiing though they are better known as Alpine skiers, with Jean-Claude Killy as their downhill icon. For cross-country skiing the French use the term *randonnée faire* (to make it [the journey on skis] out and back). *Ski de fond*, also in use, means skiing in the valley (at the bottom) rather than on the mountain slopes. A popular current term is *ski Nordique*. Yet Rossignol, the premiere French ski manufacturer, calls their most successful backcountry ski *Le Randonnée*.

*Langlaufers*, which means literally "those who run a long way," is how the Germans describe their cross-country skiers. The Swedes, who with the Norwegians have been at it longer than anyone else (4,000 years), take the *langlauf* idea a step farther. They use *langdakare* to describe those who ski a long way Stockholm-style, shuffling along on their skis as if they were wearing bedroom slippers. *Skidakare* they reserve for the more athletic skiers who extend and stride in a smooth movement they refine to a continuous glide.

The truly religious skiers in both Nordic and Alpine disciplines are the Norwegians who consistently display the greatest talent on both the high and low ground. They call cross-country skiing *langren* "long runners," and go at it with unmatched zeal. It was six brave Norwegian cross-country skiers, commandos living in the snow during World War II, who outfoxed the Germans making heavy water for a nuclear bomb at Rjukan in Norway's mountains. The Third Reich's goal was to make the first atomic bomb, and to succeed they needed this substance. By sinking the vessel ferrying the heavy water out of Norway, these commandos ended any chance Hitler had of winning the war that way. At the Lillehammer Olympics in 1996, all six men were honored at the games' opening ceremony.

While known for using hard-to-pronounce words like *murtomaahiihto*, their term for cross-country skiing, the Finns are famous for their *sisu* (guts) on skis, both at war and in Nordic competition. In their heroic Winter War with the Russians in 1939-40, and again in 1941-43, they fought on cross-country skis and even on ice skates, making sorties commando-style, demonstrating incredible initiative. They are great competitors and good sports, too. Picture the giant farmer, 6' 4" Juha Mieto, Finland's greatest skier all through the 1980s, catching up to US skier Bill Koch on a long, steep hill. He puts his hand on the tired younger skier's back and quietly intones, "*Sisu, sisu,*" pushing him all the way up the long climb before skiing past him.

Even the Brits ski—not because they are so good at it but because English gentlemen made recreational skiing fashionable at their favorite winter resorts in Europe. They coined the term "Nordic skiing" for those keen enough to ski cross-country the Norwegian way, with a loose heel. These skiing toffs, whose rigorous schooling had always extolled "a healthy mind in a healthy body," lived by that motto, *Mens sana in corpore sano*. Sir Arthur Conan Doyle was a celebrated extreme skier, "extreme" meaning here he skied "extremely dangerously." He skied both cross-country and downhill so boldly that he's well remembered for his daring rather than his skill.

*Ski de Fondo* (we're at the bottom of the mountain again) is the Italian phrase for Nordic skiing. The Italians deserve special recognition because they ski so like "dilettanti." Not amateurish, they "delight" in skiing well for the sake of doing it—the original meaning of the word. Italians love both style and speed, and Italian technology showed us how to make our skis fly. Their research into waxing in the early 1980s generated one of three quantum leaps forward in Nordic skiing during the past 25 years.

## Three Quantum Leaps in Cross-country Skiing

The first big leap was the switch from wooden to fiberglass skis; the second was the introduction of skating technique followed by its rapid development and acceptance as the new way to ski. These two innovations made cross-country skiing a faster and more attractive sport. While the new skis were great and the athletes' skating skills and fitness superb, the excellence of both raised a challenge that remained to be solved. The third leap forward, the development of new waxes, answered the question: How do you make skis interact with snow so that they achieve optimum glide? Because these three developments took place while I was trying to become a good skier and a racer on the European marathon circuit, I can offer this largely firsthand report.

In 1972 Fischer, the premiere Austrian ski manufacturer, stunned the Nordic world by putting fiberglass skis into competition with wooden skis. "*Ustortlig!*" (Unsporting!) the proud Norwegians cried. For the makers of the finest wooden racing skis, Bla-skia, this was tantamount to cheating. It was like the introduction of the aluminum baseball bat to that sport when wood had always been revered. The World Championships were held at Falun in Sweden in 1974, and only those stubborn Norwegians were still on wooden *Bla-skia* (blue skis). They blue it, while the East Germans, always willing to experiment and led by Erhart Grimmer, sucked up the medals on their Fischer fiberglass skis.

Bill Koch, aged 16, who was to become North America's only internationally acclaimed Nordic racer, skied his first race for the US team in these games, in the 4X5-km relay. Meanwhile, 17-year-old Thomas Wasberg—already the Swedish National Champion at 15 kilometers—was not allowed to ski in these games because he was being protected by his coaches from such severe competition so early in his career. He went on to win gold medals at every distance from the relay through the 15-, 30-, and 50-km events over three Olympic Games.

Traditionally, all cross-country ski racing was done with the diagonal stride. You took short, quick steps on your skis up the hills and stretched your stride out like a running chicken on the flats, while synchronizing a strong poling action with your legwork. "Diagonal stride" in skiing is derived from the term used when training horses. Your skiing action is like the quadruped's; think of your poles as two more legs. With one pole planted opposite your leading leg and the thrust off each pole diagonally opposed to the leading ski, you become a quadruped. This is how horses gallop.

No matter how skillfully you do the diagonal stride, each ski is momentarily inert when you transfer weight off it. By skating you can overcome

*Two skillful skiers skating over Royal Gorge's 9,000 acres of high Sierra territory*

David Madison/Royal Gorge

the lack-of-continuum flaw in the diagonal stride. Also, striding requires two entirely different waxes applied to your skis, one under the midsection to provide grip for stepping off (the kick wax) and another on each end for glide. Finding the right combination of waxes can be frustrating—good when it works and a nightmare when it doesn't. Skating requires one preparation for glide along the whole length of the ski. Your grip for thrust must come from the blade edge of your skis' continually cutting into the snow, not from any wax. You back up the skating action with powerful double poling so that your forward motion always has uninterrupted momentum. Skating on skis replicates ice skating with the added advantage of pole power.

When racers, using the diagonal stride, tired and their grip wax wore off, or it was no longer the right wax because of changing conditions, they were hard pressed. A technique that solved this problem called for a lot of strength. By leaving one ski in the track and gliding continuously on it, racers could skate off the other ski outside the track. They combined this with double poling, the most powerful poling technique. No need for any grip wax now. While this variation looks odd, it is exhilarating and faster than the best diagonal stride. The only questions were how long you could keep it going and were you allowed to do it?

With racers abandoning the diagonal stride, this new method, soon called the marathon skate, provided a breakthrough for cross-country skiing. The best marathon skier in the world at this time, Pauli Siitonen, "the Flying Finn," took full advantage of the method and by 1978 it was known in Europe as the "Siitonen skate." Then Bill Koch skated his way to victory in Switzerland's national marathon race, the *Engedine*, and brought his technique back to the US. It spread rapidly. Though some nations complained (those old-fashioned Norwegians again, and the Swedes), the marathon skate was allowed in competition. In fact most elite skiers used it alternately with their diagonal stride, when losing their grip, accelerating, and climbing slight gradients. Within two years all elite skiers were using at least five new ways to skate, and the breakaway from traditional skiing was complete.

Each skating method was defined by what you did with your poles—how you planted them and how you timed the planting with your leg action. Racers now skated down the middle of the trails, ignoring the set tracks and experimenting as they went, with new gears to accommodate the variations of the course and their own physical ups and downs. The international governing body for ski competition, *Federation Internationale de Ski (FIS)*, saw it would be foolish to ban skating. *FIS* wisely declared two disciplines for Nordic track competition. Classical style comprises the diagonal stride, with no skating except on corners where the skate turn would have been appropriate anyway. The new discipline is called Freestyle: do what you do best; skate your heart out.

Running my ski school when all this was happening, I was loath to give up the diagonal stride that I'd spent many years trying to perfect. But local skiers who normally finished a bit behind were now creaming me with their marathon skate. That, plus the enthusiasm of my students who were asking me to teach skating, got me into it. Within one year I could give an irrefutable measurement of its worth. Skiing in the Masters 111 category (the 50-54 age group within the international racing system for all amateur events) in 1985 I entered the annual 30-km race at Royal Gorge. Using the diagonal stride, my time of 2.04.55 was worth first place in my division. The following year, on the same course with identical conditions, I skied the whole 30 kms, using only the marathon skate. My time was 1.43.10. Skating does for skiing what swimming using its wings as oars does for a penguin. How tedious it would be for a penguin not to use its wings. Any bird with wings should at least try to fly, and anyone who skis should try skating.

In the early 1980s the Italians started winning races among the world's elite skiers. The only fast Italian on foot whom anyone could remember was Livio Barruti of Turin, who won the gold medal for 200 meters in the Rome Olympics of 1960. They had no experience of winning in competition with the best Nordic skiing nations: Norway, Sweden, Finland, East Germany, and Russia. Behind these five countries always came Czechoslovakia, consistently in sixth place in overall team results. That was before *il miracolo de fondo*, when the Italians showed up with their new waxes.

Given equally well-prepared athletes on equally well-waxed skis, the athlete with the best motor—the best heart—wins. The Italians had never had a skier like Sweden's Mora Nisse to inspire them, who won the *Vasalopp* (86 kms) nine times in ten starts, and was second by only one second in his tenth start, all in ten consecutive years. They had never had a Juha Mieto, a Thomas Wasberg, a Gundar Sven, or a Bjorn Dahli—all of whom have hearts as big as Secretariat's. While they knew that the motor comes first, as in a Ferrari, they also knew that if your motor is to win there must be friction—good wheel contact with the surface on which your Ferrari is running.

In a car race the most effective grip combined with the most power will win. Racers with power and poor grip spin their wheels. On skis it was much the same until skating became the way to ski, especially when skiing marathon distances. Skiers who glide best conserve power and need less power to win. Short on power, the Italians made it their quest to make better waxes that would reduce friction between the skis' base and the snow, and their researchers came back with the Grail.

# Nordic Skiing in the United States

How did Nordic skiing get started here and why wasn't it as popular as Alpine skiing? The basic answer to this is very simple. Americans liked to separate their recreational time from any connection with work ethics; sports stress was not their game, unless it was vicariously enjoyed as a spectator. They preferred to be towed up hills in order to ski down them. Europeans typically turned their outdoor work skills into their sports, a practice that has always been the least expensive way to fill discretionary time. Ancient Greeks set the standard for sports stress with their Olympic Games in which almost all the events were related to hunting, battle skills, or endurance. Fortunately, this American avoidance of physical fitness is no longer true. There is now great interest in arduous sporting activities, especially endurance sports with high skill levels: triathlons, biking on road and trail, cross-country skiing, windsurfing, snowboarding, rock climbing, to name a few. There is even a recreational class in America today, not based on income but on enthusiasm for physically demanding sports.

Early emigrants to the US from the three most northern Nordic countries were mostly artisans: carpenters, metal workers, farmers, etc. They came to work, bringing skills, stamina, and bread-winning work tools. There

*"Snowshoe" Thompson, California's most famous skier, looms in bronze above some contemporary Boreal snowboarders*

was no room or need to bring skis; they could make them when they got here if they relocated to the right environment. Skis were carved from mature hickory, ash, and birch trees in the local forest whether you were living in Norway, Maine, Minnesota, or California for that matter.

Scattered Nordic enclaves throughout North America's snowbound regions had families—as well as individual trappers and carriers—who snowshoed or skied. While these folk must have enjoyed the occasional skiing festival with racing, slaloming, and jumping events, there wasn't a publicly recognized recreation called Nordic or cross-country skiing in this country prior to certain developments. Americans weren't attracted to cross-country skiing in any numbers until there were destination resorts where they could stay in good hotels, skiing over fields or through woods from their lodgings.

In the late 1930s downhill skiers already had mountain resorts like Stowe in Vermont and California's fashionable Sugarbowl (Walt Disney's winter playground) built at Donner Pass. Even before Sugarbowl, the first downhill ski area in California had been developed with rope tows at Yosemite's Badger Pass, long before cross-country skiers had any commercial facilities. And the Sierra Club's Clair Tappaan Lodge at Soda Springs-Norden ran the longest rope tow in California for downhill skiers, on the west side of Donner Ski Ranch, well before a cross-country skiing program was started there.

The first Nordic destination resort in the United States was developed after World War II near Stowe, Vermont—the Trapp Family Lodge. The von Trapp family bought a farmhouse at Stowe while still touring as a singing group. When they ended their famous *Sound of Music* career, their cross-country skiing resort—on a thousand acres of lovely pastoral and wooded land—became the family project. The original farmhouse was converted into an authentic Austrian lodge. In the dining room the staff dressed in colorful dirndls. The accordion was played softly yet con brio, while Maria von Trapp visited with all her guests at their tables. It was great fun.

At various times Ned Gillet, of expedition-skiing fame, was director here of the first commercial cross-country ski school in the US. Larry Damon, who skied in four consecutive Olympics, was another director, and had several outstanding women instructors (Norwegian Olympians) on his elite staff. I trained here and was well coached by Larry, who is still running the ski school after 20 years. Because staying and skiing at this delightful lodge was like taking a holiday in Bavaria, it was distressing to hear a few years ago that it had been destroyed by fire. However, a new lodge was built and I have heard that the quality of this New England program is undiminished. In fact there are now 2,200 acres to ski.

Two other cross-country skiing resorts have had a huge impact on the growth of the sport in this country. They are the Telemark Resort in Wisconsin, and California's Royal Gorge, in the Tahoe-Donner Region. You can fly into the Telemark Resort in your own Learjet and land right in front of your hotel accommodation. It's a four-season resort that has everything the private individual or the large corporate conference group could want. After returning from the Korean War, Tony Wise embarked on his remarkable entrepreneurial career by creating this sophisticated outdoor-recreation center. He brought in Bill Koch to design the 50 kilometers of challenging ski trails on the 2,000-acre property. He also started the most successful marathon ski race in the US, a wildly popular event named the American Birkebeiner. (The original *Birkebeiner* race in Norway celebrates the ancient skiers who wore "birch-bark leggings" to protect themselves from the snow. They were good guys who overcame the *Baglers* (bad guys) in 1206 by carrying the child Hakon Hakonsson 58 kilometers from Lillehammer to Nidaros where they convinced King Inge to accept him as rightful heir to the Norwegian throne.)

In his *Cross-Country Ski Vacations: A Guide to the Best Resorts, Lodges, and Groomed Trails in North America,* Jonathan Wiesel described Tony Wise as "a visionary and perhaps the greatest promoter the sport has ever known." He was not referring to North America alone because the World Loppet, a series of marathon races held wherever recreational skiing has a good footing, was another of Tony's brainstorms. There are World Loppet events in Europe, Canada, the United States, Japan, and Australia, where the Aussies ruefully call their race the Kangaroo Hoppit. For a while Wisconsin's Tony Wise was "Emperor" of North American Nordic skiing. Unfortunately, like King Gordius whose wheels fell off his cart when Alexander the Great conquered Phrygia, Tony's wheels fell off his wagon when the banks foreclosed on him. Yet his Birkebeiner race is still the blue-ribbon event for cross-country's Great American Ski Chase, the series of regional marathon races across the US that recognize champions in every age group.

I flew to Telemark in September, 1978 as Tony Wise's guest to interview for the job of Ski School Director. For two days I ran the trails, ate excellent meals, and enjoyed a comfortable suite while waiting for him to get back from his latest bank conference. At 2 A.M. on the third morning I was summoned to Tony's office. By 5 A.M. I'd heard his life story and had shaken hands with him; I had the job. The following day I learned that the current ski school director didn't know he'd been fired. So, I declined the job, moved to California, and started the ski school at the Sierra Club's Clair Tappaan Lodge.

My neighbors at Soda Springs were developing Royal Gorge, which has since become the biggest privately owned cross-country skiing resort in the world. John Slouber and Jonathan Wiesel were in harness, practically pulling the track setters themselves. They split up and, 20 years later under Slouber's direction, the Royal Gorge Cross Country Ski Resort has an unrivaled mileage of machine-groomed trails (more than 300 kms) on 9,000 acres of richly forested land. They also have one of the largest subalpine meadows in California, on what was formerly Lake Van Norden.

Royal Gorge offers the widest variety of Nordic facilities anywhere. There are five complete trail systems and four surface lifts strategically placed to assist tired skiers heading home, and offer skiers maximum enjoyment practicing downhill techniques, particularly telemarking. There is the comfortable Wilderness Lodge, accessed by a 5-kilometer sleigh ride, and a first-class country hotel, the Rainbow Lodge on Interstate 80. Royal Gorge is also the venue for the final event in the Great American Ski Chase. Each year this race is held in conjunction with Royal Gorge's own ski festival, in which the California Gold Rush (50 kms), the Silver Rush (30 kms), and the Bronze Rush (15 kms) are the main events.

While the Trapp Family Lodge, the Telemark Resort, and the Royal Gorge Resort are the benchmark programs, there are now numerous other outstanding cross-country skiing resorts across the United States. Several of the best are in California. It's fair to say that Nordic skiing—no longer a Cinderella sport in the US—is alive and very well in the Far West.

# Nordic Skiing and Racing in College Programs

Nordic skiing and racing programs in American colleges have had a profound influence on the high standards that are noticeable at resorts. Besides cross-country skiing, Nordic skiing embraces jumping events and the biathlon, in which skiers demonstrate their shooting skills at stations along their racing route. Only college programs could find enough good skiers willing to participate in these more esoteric and expensive Nordic events. New Hampshire, Vermont, and Colorado are the states with the most successful college ski teams. Maria von Trapp's son, Johannes, whose seminar on ski-resort management introduced me to the Trapp Family Lodge, was educated at Dartmouth, where all the skiing disciplines have been well coached for years.

Dartmouth, Middlebury, the University of Vermont, and The Putney School—the prep school in Vermont, where John Caldwell coached Bill Koch and many other future Olympians—became the first nurseries for Nordic racing in the United States. For many years it was from these schools that almost all the US Olympic teams' cross-country skiers graduated. When these and other college racers moved on they took their high level of performance with them, teaching skills and spreading their own enthusiasm for the sport. One of these Olympians, Peter Davis, even started his own Nordic prep school in Vermont. In the Far West Region, which includes Arizona and Nevada, the University of Nevada at Reno, and the University of Alaska now play a similar role in setting high Nordic performance standards. These high standards permeate the sport through the young college racers who can be seen competing in Citizen skiing events throughout California.

≈

How does racing affect the rest of us—the slower, recreational skiers? We've benefited from the design breakthroughs I've described. There are now well-groomed trails at cross-country resorts, with ski schools often directed by former elite college racers (the best skiers in America). For many, the novelty and excitement brought into recreational skiing by competition skaters has become the most compelling aspect of the sport. These days everyone wants to try skating. Even downhill skiers—jaded by repetitious runs down the same old slopes—want to skate cross-country.

Improvements in equipment and in warm, lightweight clothing are available to all. Designed first to meet the racers' needs, they are then passed on to us. In fact, every new idea developed at the top end of the sport and found satisfactory is on the market for recreational skiers within a year. Even the magic new waxes can be bought in stores—like Paco's Bike & Ski in Truckee—that specialize in helping their racing clients. But you'll have to pay a lot for such high-end products.

On buying the trail pass at cross-country ski areas, we weekend skiers become lottery winners. We ski on trails groomed to competition standards because the machines are the same as those made for competition grooming. We use skis, boots, and poles whose prototypes were made to meet the demands of elite skiers. Our skiing techniques come to us from the racing perfectionists, and are modified by ski instructors for our recreation needs. And there's recreation equipment the racers don't have: non-wax skis for beginners at diagonal-stride skiing, and much shorter skis for novices to help them skate, turn, and stop. John Slouber at Royal Gorge has worked with both Fischer and

Salomon (ski boots), while Paul Petersen at Bear Valley has worked with Rossignol, helping these elite manufacturers address the needs of first-time skiers—skiers who must be comfortable on their equipment on day one or they won't come back.

People who have not yet been cross-country skiing often ask why ski on a groomed trail when the sport is called cross-country. The cross-country skiing public falls into self-selecting groups. There are those—not many—who want to stay off the groomed trails. Yet these wilderness skiers often make tracks close to groomed trails because of the security they provide. Then there are the telemarkers who ski the backcountry as well as lift-operated areas. Finally, there are the happy, groomed-trail skiers. Most cross-country skiers prefer and need machine-groomed areas, not only for their safety but so they can glide. Gliding is far more easily achieved on snow that's been packed and had all the wrinkles smoothed out by machines. Both safety and glide are particularly important if parents want to include their children. Many areas in this book have supervised snow play for small children so parents can take off to ski. Another important convenience for weekend skiers is that equipment can be rented at all the areas. And there are bathrooms, refreshments, and rest areas.

## Learn to Ski by Taking Lessons

Before the satisfaction of gliding smoothly along groomed trails can be enjoyed, the beginner will want to learn how to ski. If you want to learn how to stop and turn without falling down, or stride or skate proficiently, there is always some professional instruction available at groomed areas. You cannot learn these skills more easily than in a controlled situation, a situation that only the groomed resort provides. Most ski schools have competent instructors, many of whom have been coached by the best certified instructors on the West Coast such as Debbi Waldear, Nancy Fiddler, Paul Petersen, Glenn Jobe, and others I will mention in subsequent chapters of this book.

All the ski areas in this book have machine-groomed trails. (We owe a lot to the grooming crews who work all night so that we can play the next day.) The resorts have comfortable facilities, which provide the opportunity for social contact if you want company. When skiers get cold or tired there are base lodges with food and hot drinks to return to, and along the trails there are warming huts.

# 2   Getting Started

## Getting There

Assuming you are in good health—chat with your doctor first if you're not sure—we can talk about how you get to the snow. From as far away as Alaska, New York, and Florida, people fly into Reno, rent 4WD vehicles at the airport, and drive to the Lake Tahoe Region. The cross-country skiing is that good in California, and the season is long. Bay Area folk can take a bus up to Soda Springs and walk or hitch a lift 3 or 4 miles up Donner Pass Road to the Sierra Club's Clair Tappaan Lodge or the Donner Spitz Hutte for the least expensive weekend skiing trip.

If you are of the majority, neither likely to fly nor take the bus, you need a 4WD vehicle or a reliable car with a good set of snow chains. Learn to put these chains on before you leave home, rather than on the road in a snowstorm. If you cannot manage the chains, there are chain-on-and-off stations at Interstate 80 interchanges, on each side of the heavy snowfall area. In a number of California ski resort regions, where mountain passes have to be negotiated, such as Kirkwood, Bear Valley, Yosemite, and Kings Canyon, it is mandatory to carry snow chains throughout the winter. You can be ticketed in these areas if you are caught without them. You need to know the road conditions ahead of time, and with Yosemite and Kings Canyon you should consider the best part of the season for you to drive there. (Late-season snowstorms stymied me twice this season before reaching Yosemite to ski from Badger Pass to Glacier Point.)

The biggest cross-country ski area of them all, Royal Gorge, near I-80 on the west side of Squaw Ridge and Donner Summit, can almost always be reached without serious delays due to weather conditions. Another outstanding Nordic area just outside Truckee, Tahoe Donner Cross Country, also doesn't involve the long drive to Lake Tahoe. If you want to go skiing give enough thought to your logistics first.

## Where To Stay—Contingency Lodging

In the Area Chapters of this book, I describe where I've been comfortable. I also indicate the many lodging and restaurant options close to each cross-country skiing resort. It is worth noting other lodgings along your route you can fall back to if you encounter adverse weather. For instance, Fresno is the obvious place to wait out a storm for Kings Canyon. Or if you're beyond Fresno on Hwy. 180, Squaw Valley (not the Lake Tahoe version) or Grant Grove becomes your fallback. The Priests House, right on your route to Yosemite, is a good stopover in bad weather; it's isolated but has a restaurant. For the Tahoe Region, when you're driving west on I-80, the inexpensive Colfax Motor Lodge has long been my fallback lodging. I've had to use all three of these emergency accommodations. When driving north to the Shasta Nordic Center, Dunsmuir—near the mountain but at a much lower elevation—would be my refuge in a snowstorm.

## Clothing & Outfitting for Cross-country Skiing

Unlike for downhill skiing, for cross-country you need light clothing because you are always generating body heat with your activity. Choose clothing carefully to protect you without overheating you. Choose underclothing that absorbs sweat, a lightweight but warm mid-layer, and a lightweight, totally windproof outer garment. This should be a breathable, waterproof shell. For pants, ordinary running tights make a great base layer. To go over those, the Reebok windproof pants, lined for warmth on cold days or unlined for milder conditions, are ideal. (An absolute bargain at the price, I wear them year-round.)

If you're skiing competitively or training hard, you'll want close-fitting, lightweight clothing—probably a Lycra bodysuit. It's warm enough while you're generating a lot of heat, but don't forget warmer clothing for your start and finish. Unhurried skiers can afford to wear loser, warmer clothing allowing some air circulation. At an outdoor adventure sports store, find a salesperson who knows cross-country skiing and take it from there. In California's urban areas, R.E.I. and similar stores can take care of you. In all of the Lake Tahoe Region there's not a better store for every facet of cross-country skiing than Paco's Bike & Ski in Truckee. Or if you're near the lake, Alpenglow in Tahoe City is worth a visit. If you are up at Mt. Shasta and need any cross-country clothing or equipment, The Fifth Season has it. (See Appendix 1)

I include under clothing several items you must have as a cross-country skier. A fanny pack and a lightweight backpack are essential; you'll always need one or the other and maybe both. Have a water bottle or two with you, because you need to replace body fluids all the time while skiing. You can dehydrate easily without noticing it, until it becomes painfully obvious. Use sunglasses and buy good ones that won't harm your eyes. Sunblock and lip balm should be applied before you set out—not as an afterthought. And finally, you need gloves. If you are not used to the cold, you should have a pair of warm, loose-fitting, knitted gloves or mittens. For vigorous skiing, you need close-fitting cross-country gloves designed to help you hold your ski poles correctly. These gloves are more of a sheath to prevent blisters than to keep your hands warm. You may need to wear heavier gloves over them while skiing.

## Cross-country Skiing Equipment

If you are a beginner, rent, rent, rent. You should rent at least three times and try out different boots and skis before you invest several hundred dollars on a complete outfit of skis, boots, bindings, and poles. Be aware that most boots are designed to match a particular binding to hold them to the ski: only that one binding will work with that boot. As for skis, the range to chose from is very wide.

Before you decide what skis to buy, be sure you know your goal as a skier, because the technical differences that determine a ski's performance—apart from your performance—also determine its price range. Skis alone range in price from $100 to $400 or more. If you intend to become a good skier, spending a lot of time on your skis, it won't hurt to start out with superior equipment. But if you do that, it matters even more that you rent first, to find out what works best for you. When you can appreciate the difference between one make of ski and another, and choose the best boot and binding combina-

*Every length and design of Fischer skis are available for rent at Royal Gorge*

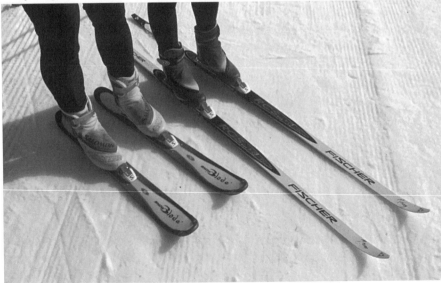

David Madison/Royal Gorge

tion and the best poles for you, then is the time to invest in topflight equipment. Of course, some people who can barely drive insist on buying a Ferrari for their first car—probably a bright red one—and good luck to them.

I can think of a dozen manufacturers who make good skis; in fact I've skied on equipment made by every one of them. While they all make reliable touring skis, only a few make technically superior skis. Of these I'll name what I have in my own racing locker, all of which have to be waxed: Fischer, Atomic, Rossignol, and Karhu. For telemarking and backcountry skiing I like lightweight equipment and prefer Fischer's E 99 with the Salomon backcountry boot and binding. Rossignol makes a good combination with the entire boot, binding, and ski package designed by them. If you want to try out Rossignol equipment, you can't do better than to visit Paul Petersen's program at Bear Valley. Just as John Slouber has worked with Fischer and Salomon to develop rental equipment for Royal Gorge, Paul has done the same with Rossignol.

If you are an occasional cross-country skier who enjoys track skiing (and that's how most people start out, skiing a few weekends each season), be sure to rent first. When you do buy, you'll probably be best off with skis that don't need a grip wax underfoot. There are many companies making low-maintenance skis with a milled configuration under the foot that give you a reliable grip on all snow conditions except ice. Among these are Track, Alpina, Asne, and Madhus. All such skis are for striding; they are not for skating. While you can try skating on them, they do not glide well enough for that technique. Skating skis are more refined and will cost more. They require much longer poles because the poling action for skating is so different from that for striding.

The one piece of equipment that tends to be of poor quality in most rental programs is the item you're most likely to break—your poles. While they are your weakest tools, they're the ones you rely on to prop you up. Ask for longer rather than shorter poles; they keep you upright. And when you get around to buying poles, get good ones. Though telemarking is best done with shorter poles, striding requires long, shoulder-height poles. When you're serious about skating, you'll want poles as high as your nose (up to your chin when starting out).

*Occasional and intermediate skiers do not need to purchase the sort of equipment used by elite skiers. Serious skiers, like any athlete in training, will want the best. Rent equipment until you're sure what to buy and take ski lessons to help you decide what to buy. Lessons are a really good idea because your instructor gets to see how you ski and is better able to advise you than a salesperson, who may have only your enthusiasm and pocketbook to go on.*

## What To Carry with You

Just as you don't set out on a cross-country driving trip with an empty tank, don't go out on the trails hungry or thirsty. Hot and cold drinks and snacks are available at all groomed ski areas. Often they have a buffet with hot soups and chili, as well as a range of carbohydrates. *You should never go out on the trails hungry or thirsty, because there's probably no outdoor recreation that burns calories and body fluids faster than cross-country skiing.* If you start out low on fuel, expect an empty tank very soon. Carbohydrates are your best fuel.

Apart from what's available at the ski lodge, you should carry snacks and never start out without a bottle full of water or a fruit drink. In the long run fluids are even more important than snacks, and all snacks of the Power Bar variety need to be drunk with water if they are to give you any energy boost. Instructions on the packages tell you this, but many people don't read them and wonder why they get indigestion instead of the charge they were expecting. Drink up!

## Warm Clothing

Unless conditions are as perfect as they often are in California and you know your route exactly—how long it will take you to ski out and return—take extra clothing to warm up when you get cold. Typically, you get cold when you take a break or when you've been out quite a while and are getting tired. Have a windbreaker and either a warm vest or jersey on or in your day pack. When you take a break put something chill-proof on; even on a sunny day a light breeze carries a chill factor that you may not notice until you're cold.

It's worth noting what I carried and how I carried it, when I skied alone from Badger Pass to Glacier Point and back, 34 kms (21 miles). This was not backcountry skiing. I was on an unplowed road using nonwax touring skis and averaging 4 mph. There was no chance I would meet another skier because the area was officially closed for the season. (I had permission to be there.) For my safety I had to carry a lot. Had I been on skating skis with fast conditions, and known that other skiers would be on the trail, I would have needed only two, full water bottles. In 2.5 hours I'd have been there and back with no need to carry any extra clothing. (Speed is warmth.) As it was, I had plenty of extra clothing, food, and fluids. I carried it all in two lightweight packs. The trip took me almost 8 hours there and back, which was way over my anticipated time.

Whatever your skiing ability is, you should carry whatever you might need to ward off cold or exhaustion. That you have paid to ski on groomed trails at a privately owned and well-operated ski area doesn't relieve you of responsibility for your own comfort or safety. While you usually start out from a warm ski lodge or your own car, you have to ask yourself where you'll be in two hours time. Far from a warming hut, you may want that jacket, jersey, or an energy boost that's in your pack.

## Carry a Map

You're unlikely to need a compass at a groomed ski area, though it might be fun to carry one along to see if you can relate it to your map. Without exception, all professionally run cross-country ski areas in California have detailed maps of all their trails. These maps are free, and should be offered to you whenever you purchase a trail pass. If you are not offered one, ask for one. Unless you know the area you are skiing well, you should always carry one of the resort's maps. All trails are posted with their names, letters, or numbers, and often show distances to the base lodge. At most areas the trails are color-coded as well; practice locating your position on your map. All maps indicate each trail's scale of difficulty from a novice's point of view so you can choose trails to challenge you or trails to avoid.

*This is the perfect age for children to be learning to ski, as these two are at Royal Gorge. No need for ski poles yet.*

David Madison/Royal Gorge

# 3 Three Ways To Cross-country Ski

## Classical

The diagonal stride, or just "striding," is the classical way of skiing cross-country; it is officially referred to this way in competition from the local level to the Olympics. While use of the word "diagonal" is slowly slipping away from common usage, all coaches use it to define the physical relationship of legs to arms when a skier is striding on the tracks. What is diagonal is the imaginary line drawn through the foot on the lead ski to the basket on the pole that the skier pushes off on. Ski coaches applied the term from equitation to skiing after relating the skier's motions to the same diagonal action in a horse's opposite leg movements.

The diagonal stride is walking or running on your skis while using a pole in each hand to give you added propulsion down the trail. As a beginner walking on your skis, rather than trying to pick your ski up off the snow, you lift your heel and slide that foot forward with each step. While the toe of your boot is attached to the ski by its binding, your heel is completely free to rise off the ski. Otherwise you could not walk but only drag and slide.

While striding, instead of just swinging your arms forward and backward as if hiking, you raise a ski pole, plant it opposite your lead foot, and push down on it to help propel you forward. This part of your skiing movement is called "poling." If you plant both poles ahead of you to push down on them simultaneously it's called "double poling." Use double poling alone when the glide is so good that you don't need to take steps.

As you progress, your walking style on skis extends to a delightfully smooth stride. There is a flowing synergism of all four limbs, which the Swedes

## Six Good Turns for the Cross-country Skier

2. Snowplow Turn

1. Step Turn

*3. Skate Turn*

*5. Telemark Turn on skating skis*

*6. Tiptoe Turn*

*Stem Turn on E 99 backcountry skis*

*Telemark Turn on*
*E 99 backcountry skis*

*Double image of Paul Petersen from Bear Valley
demonstrating the diagonal stride*

call *"skidakare"* (ski running). It is analogous to a swimmer's leg kicks well coordinated with good arm strokes. The good swimmer and the good skier seem to glide effortlessly when they've mastered their techniques. Both have overcome the body's confusion on being asked to do several different things powerfully, smoothly, and simultaneously. If you get to this stage as a skier, those who know will note approvingly that you have a "classic diagonal stride."

## Freestyle

In the Nordic world freestyle skiing doesn't mean doing tricks in the air or bouncing over the moguls; it means skating instead of striding. It's a faster way to ski, which most people feel is more exciting. Especially among racers it has become the preferred way to ski cross-country. Beyond that, it gives women a better chance to use their superior leg strength without having to rely on arm strength. And you no longer have to mess with the business of applying the right grip wax under the middle of your ski. While there are different glide waxes for different conditions, now you can wax the whole ski with just one hard wax.

Because skating on skis is like being on a very long pair of ice skates, if you are an ice skater, inline skater, or even a roller skater, the crossover to skis is almost automatic. You have two aids on skis that don't exist on skates: your two poles and the broad flat bottoms of your skis. Skating on skis you glide on the flat of one ski, while you cut into the snow and push off with the other's edge. The snow-cutting or skating ski propels you on the firm platform of the gliding ski. It feels magical.

Supporting the magic is the physics. No matter how well you ski the diagonal stride, when—after stepping forward—your weight comes down on your rear ski that ski is inert on the snow. On completing the step you bring the rear ski forward and it resumes its propulsion, but a loss of momentum has occurred. Yet there is never a moment when skating that both skis aren't moving forward. The diagonal stride is less efficient, and this can be expressed by two simple equations: in skating, Mass plus Speed = Momentum; in striding, Loss of Momentum = Loss of Speed. *Quod erat demonstrandum* (which was to be proved).

# Downhill

Downhill performance is the main concern of every newcomer to cross-country skiing. If you're used to lift-skiing at downhill resorts, keep in mind that with skinny skis you have to apply your weight to your ski edges very purposefully. These skis need more than the slight encouragement you have to give downhill skis to make turns. For those people who have never skied, the term "fall line" may sound ominous, but it simply refers to the direction that water would flow if you turned a tap on at any given point on a hill. Whether a hill's gradient is slight or steep, the term is used. Yet the beginner's concern is how to avoid careening gravity-impelled down the fall line. You avoid this either by setting your skis as brakes rather than as gliders, or by weaving them back and forth across the fall line.

Turning on your skis, decreasing speed, and stopping are intrinsically connected, with one proviso. The snowplow (wedge) method, used for slowing down while continuing down the fall line, can be applied forcefully enough to bring you to a standstill only on a moderate downhill slope. Where it's steep, to stop you are either going to make a sitzmark (a backward fall) or a turn. (Don't be ashamed of your sitzmark—it got you out of trouble.) If you're using a wedge and it's not slowing you, convert it to a turn by weighting the inside edge of the ski that's pointing the way you want to go. By completing the turn across and slightly into the hill, you'll come to a standstill. Make an abrupt turn across your line of progress to stop quickly. To slow down using turns, switchback repeatedly across the fall line. (Out of control and don't know what to do? Sit down!)

# Six Easy Turns

In cross-country skiing there are *Five Easy Turns.*\* I'm going to describe them (adding one more for fun) with a sequence of illustrative photos by Daphne Hougard. They are the step, snowplow, skate, stem, telemark, and tiptoe turns. As the photos show, the skate turn progresses from the step turn, just as the stem turn does from the snowplow. These first four turns, well executed, will make you a competent and safe downhill skier on cross-country equipment.

Telemarks and tiptoes are stylish turns that you can learn when you have mastered the other four. The only exclusively Nordic turn, the telemark, can't be skied without a free heel; it will establish you as a better skier. The tiptoe is a playful, sixth-sense turn that adds character to your skiing. By reducing your fear of falling, knowing how to turn and stop before you cut loose will greatly enhance your skiing enjoyment. While all turns, completed so that they take you toward the hill, can be used to stop, the step, skate, and tiptoe turns can be applied in multiples. The stem, snowplow, and telemark turns can stop you by simply applying them

David Madison/Royal Gorge

*A veteran Royal Gorge skier skates powerfully uphill on the Palisade Peak Track System*

with force. Although the following brief descriptions (cross-referenced with the photos following p. 18) can serve as your introduction or review, if you want to become a competent and safe skier on cross-country equipment, take lessons.

## 1. Step Turn

This most basic turn for cross-country skiing is not unlike walking around a corner. First lift the front of the inside ski and point it where you want to turn, leaving its tail on the snow. While doing this, your weight is on the flat of the outside, gliding ski. Transfer weight to the inside ski and bring the outside ski in line with it. Take as many steps as you need to change direction. If necessary, maintain momentum by pushing with you poles, which also serve as outriggers.

## 2. Snowplow Turn

First position your skis in a wedge (or inverted "V") shape. Place your weight equally on the inside edges of both skis. Keep the ski tips about 6″ apart and the tails as wide apart as possible. You can use this position to slow down or stop on a hill. If you keep moving in this position, you can turn by shifting your weight: by more heavily weighting the inside edge of your left ski, you'll turn right, and vice versa. The more weight you apply to the inside edge of one ski, the more it will turn for you—in the direction it's pointing. The secret is holding the wedge shape of your skis no matter how you shift your weight.

## 3. Skate Turn

This progression from the slower step turn begins with bending your outside knee (farthest from the intended turn) and putting all your weight on that ski's inside edge before driving off it into an accelerated form of the step turn. The compression afforded by bending that knee creates a dynamic momentum used by racers to accelerate through flat and shallow downhill turns.

## 4. Stem Turn

Initiate a snowplow by stemming (reducing) speed with the inside edge of the ski on the outside of the turn. As soon as you start to turn, plant the trailing uphill pole on the inside of your turn, and ski around it by fully weighting the outside ski and bringing the inside ski beside it. Now, share your weight between the skis on their uphill edges. A 6″ gap between the skis when parallel adds to your stability.

## 5. Telemark Turn

(I am describing the "classical" telemark, not the tough telemark or "Norpine," which was developed by alpine skiers wearing heavyweight cross-country gear.) Weight the leading ski on its inside edge and drive it with your foot and bent knee through the turn. While the inside edge of the lead ski carves the turn, drop your rear knee over the trailing ski, weighting its outside edge slightly with your little toe. Not only preventing the rear ski from jagging across the snow and perhaps spoiling the turn, by extending the length of your carving edges this maneuver helps finesse it. By alternately switching your leading leg, you can link a series of telemark turns.

## 6. Tiptoe Turn

I developed this turn for both fun and utility and have seen no one else teach anything like it. It's useful for a quick change of direction with minimal loss of momentum on flats and easy downhill stretches. Torque your upper body in the direction you want to turn, and swing both poles ahead to form a gate. As your poles meet the ground, lift your body weight so that you can pop your ski tips up on the snow, pivoting on your tails, into the gate. While the tiptoe is easy to approximate, it requires perfect timing to be effective. For fun and exhilaration use them for short-swing downhill runs in 6″ of fresh powder or on corn snow in the spring.

\* *Five Easy Turns* was an instructional book describing the five basic turns that cross-country skiers need on downhill slopes. Tom Martens, editor of the *Tahoe World* newspaper, and I were the authors.

*John Stoddart, chief guide at the Royal Gorge Wilderness Lodge, telemarking*

David Madison/Royal Gorge

# 4   Swedish Drill

Recommended before and after any major physical exertion by physicians, physical therapists, coaches, and friends who do it, stretching is one of life's few panaceas. And yet it's easy to forget unless you make it a habit. For 25 years I've used a daily suite of eight exercises, with one stretch repeated between each and another to wrap up. I credit stretching with letting me at age 65 participate in long-distance ocean kayak races and marathon cross-country ski races. I'm not training vigorously for the World Masters Championships; it's simply a way of life.

   This set of exercises was known as Swedish Drill when I was introduced to it in basic training as a Royal Marine in Britain. Each exercise emphasizes four elements: extension while in motion, continuity of movement, balance, and stamina. I also emphasize composure during the exercise repetitions. Learn the correct form of each exercise before concentrating on doing many. There's nothing frenetic, exhausting, or high impact about them. Because their essential theme is rhythm and extension, I like to listen to classical music when I do them, particularly Vivaldi. There's always a tempo that's just right for me with Antonio Vivaldi; for timing and inspiration I encourage you to find your own maestro.

## Two Stretches & Eight Strengthening Exercises

(Refer to the accompanying photos as you read the following descriptions. Choose your own number of repetitions and increase them only as you improve. The numbers here are based on my own fitness program. The exercises take me 40 minutes daily.)

## S-1. One-leg Stand Stretch (to be done at intervals between exercises)

Daphne Hougard

Stand up straight on one leg. Grasp the ankle of the other foot and pull it up to your buttock. Maintaining your ankle grasp, bend forward from the waist and hold the position for at least a count of 10. Lower the ankle to the ground as you straighten up. Repeat the exercise standing on your other leg. There is no loss of benefit if you hold onto something for support. When you're thoroughly warmed up, try the unsupported position in the third image.

## 1. Full Arm Circling

Daphne Hougard

Standing with one leg slightly in front for balance, swing your fully extended arms together describing circles—10 times backward, 10 times forward—but not too fast. Do up to 5 cycles for 100 total repetitions. (Remember to do the one-leg stand between exercises.)

## 2. Touch the Ground—Reach for the Sky

Daphne Hougard

Standing with your feet wide apart, bend slowly from the waist to touch the ground. Then, slowly straighten from the waist and reach for the sky with your fingertips extended. Lower your arms to your sides. Repeat the exercise up to 20 times. Smoothness and extension are what count. (Followed by the one-leg stand.)

## 3. Downhill Squat and Arm Swing

Daphne Hougard

With your feet and knees no more than 4" apart, squat so that your lower leg and thigh form as close to a right angle at the knee (as close as you can get) while keeping your balance. Now, swing both your arms together fully extended forward, backward, and forward again (rhythm rather than speed is important). Since this is not an easy exercise, begin with about 10 repetitions and gradually work up to as many as 100. (Followed by the one-leg stand.)

## 4. Windmill Arm Swing

Daphne Hougard

With your feet fairly wide apart, bend low (about 90°) from the waist and, with your arms forming the opposing blades of a windmill, swing one hand to its opposite foot while the other arm swings skyward. Rotate your torso at the waist both ways for up to 100 repetitions. If you're stiff, start slowly and let your hands fall short of your toes. (Followed by the one-leg stand.)

## 5. Around the World with Trunk and Arms

Daphne Hougard

With your legs wide apart and your arms extended together, draw a full circle around your axis with your hands. Keep your right leg straight as you bend your left knee to touch your left foot with both hands. Now, straighten your left leg as you rise, sweeping your hands in a wide arc up and—with a hollow back—over your head. Keep your hands traveling through their arc and, as they go down, bend your right knee so you can touch your right foot. Brush your toes with your fingers each time. Keep the whole movement flowing smoothly. Begin by circling with your hands 5 times in each direction, and later working up to 10 circles each way. (Followed by the one-leg stand.)

## 6. Arm Swing and Head Frame

With feet apart and hands crossed in front of your body, swing your arms up horizontally and then let them fall back to the hands-crossed position. Repeat this 20 times with a vigorous rhythm. Complete the exercise by swinging your arms up and over your head to frame it. Do this from 10 to 20 times before reverting to the horizontal arm movement for another 20 repetitions. Do not rise on your toes while doing this exercise. (Followed by the one-leg stand.)

## 7. Racing Breast Stroke

Starting with both elbows raised high and fingertips touching in front of your chest, reach out as far in front as you can before bringing your hands back toward your chest (as if you were swimming the breast stroke). Keep your elbows high except when your hands are turning to make the next stroke. Swim up to 100 strokes, maintaining good form throughout. (Followed by the one-leg stand.)

## 8. Horizontal Arm and Shoulder Rotation

With feet about 1' apart, look to your left and reach out horizontally left with your left arm, simultaneously bringing your right arm across your chest with your hand touching your left shoulder. Fix that position for a moment and then rotate your whole upper body to the right so that your right elbow moves 270°, with your left arm and head rotating as far as they can. Keep your elbows up, arms horizontal to the ground, and feet stationary. With arms in the opposite position, rotate left. Do up to 30 rotations each way, totaling 60.

## S-2. The Camel's Back Stretch (to be done after the suite of eight exercises)

Kneel with straight arms extending vertically to the ground supported by closed fists (for less strain on your wrists). Without letting your feet slip back, slowly raise your rump by straightening your legs. Stay in this position for as long as you like, before lowering yourself back to the kneeling position. Now, hollow your back and look up. Hold this position for several seconds before raising your rump again to form the camel's back. Repeat.

# Area 1—At a Glance

## Shasta Ski Park Cross Country Center
104 Siskiyou Ave., Mt. Shasta, CA 96067
(530) 754-7427                    www.skipark.com

### Distance From
Bay Area—295 mi.    Stockton—265 mi.    Sacramento—245 mi.
Reno—220 mi.        Davis—210 mi.       Chico—135 mi.

### Elevation, Facilities, & Hours
Trails—5,245-5,560'     Groomed—31 kms      Telemark—4 lifts
Warming huts—1          Dogs—1 trail
Snowshoeing—1 trail     Hours—9 A.M.-4 P.M.

### Passes & Rental Prices

|                   | Adult (18-59) | Jr./Sr. (13-17/60-69) | Child (7-12) |
|-------------------|---------------|-----------------------|--------------|
| Trail pass        | $16           | $14                   | $9           |
| Skis, boots, poles| $12           | $12                   | $6           |
| Snowshoes         | $15           | -                     | -            |
| Pulk sled         | $20           | -                     | -            |

### Ski School

|                   | Adult (18-59) | Jr. (13-17) | Sr./Child (60-69)/(7-12) |
|-------------------|---------------|-------------|--------------------------|
| Full package (includes 90-min. group lesson, equipment rental, trail pass) | $35 | $35 | $29 |

Group track or skating lesson, 90 minutes $15.
Private lesson, 1 hour $30; each additional person $15.
**Tiny Tracks Snow School:** ages 5-9 years, weekends, and holidays only, 2-hour morning or afternoon; one session $25, both sessions $40.

### Lodging & Food
McCloud—5 miles east, or Shasta City—5 miles west, of the junction with Hwy. 89. Call Shasta Chamber of Commerce (530) 926-4865.

### Ski Shop
The Fifth Season in Shasta sells all cross-country gear and clothing. Call (530) 926-3606.

# 5   Northern California
# Mount Shasta

## AREA 1. SHASTA SKI PARK CROSS COUNTRY CENTER

### Summary

Shasta Ski Park Cross Country Center has 31 kms of groomed trails with set tracks for classical stride and a wide skating lane. Telemark skiing is lift-served 1 mile north at the Snow Park Downhill Skiing Area. Lessons for all skills are available. All trails are wide with some flat and some undulating ones. This is an ideal area for first-timers and intermediate skiers. There is a long groomed trail used by snowshoers and dog handlers. Accommodations are plentiful in Mt. Shasta and McCloud, each of which is 10 miles from the ski area in opposite directions.

### How to get there

*From the Bay Area* take I-80 35 miles east to the junction with I-505 in Vacaville. Drive north on I-505 to I-5 and continue north as described, below. *From Sacramento* take I-5 north to the junction with Hwy. 89 (0.5 mile short of Mt. Shasta). Turn right (east) toward McCloud and drive 5 miles to the SHASTA SKI PARK sign. Turn left (north) onto USFS Road 88. This minor road leads 5 miles to the Shasta Ski Park Cross Country Center parking lot, on the left side of the road. The lodge, behind the parking lot, isn't visible from the road. The alpine lifts of Shasta Ski Park—for telemark skiing—are 1 mile north of the Nordic Center. *From Reno* take Hwy. 395 north to Susanville. Head west on Hwy. 44 to

31

Old Station. Turn right (north) onto Hwy. 89 and drive to USFS Road 88 (5 miles short of the junction with I-5). Turn right and continue as above. *From Chico* drive 40 miles north on Hwy. 99 to Red Bluff, then north on I-5 to Hwy. 89 and proceed as described above.

## Special driving advice

Highway 89, linking Mt. Shasta with McCloud, is a heavily used timber-hauling road. Logging trailers are slow climbers; don't tailgate them, and overtake them with caution. USFS Road 88 may be icier after snowplowing than the highway leading to it. **Either have chains with you or drive a 4WD vehicle.**

## Description of skiing area

The Cross Country Center is 10 miles equidistant from Mt. Shasta and McCloud. While it is one of the lower elevation ski areas in California, it's in a good snowbelt. Only 1 mile north are Mt. Shasta's lower slopes, which support a mountain mass towering 14,168 feet over the northern part of the state. Shasta is never more impressive than in winter when it reaches skyward from the trails you are skiing on.

The small lodge, managed by Karen Aldous, has a cozy atmosphere. As you get your trail pass, rent your equipment, sign up for lessons or tours, or get advice before setting off on your own, you'll find the staff friendly. There is even one long trail groomed for you and your dog, and for snowshoers. A charming warming hut built like a little temple (called the Temple Hut) awaits you at 5,560 feet, the highest point on the trails. Benches and picnic tables are situated at several open places along the trails. In the lodge you can have hot tea or coffee, and hot soups are also available.

From the perspective of a newcomer to cross-country skiing, the quality of the grooming, wide width of the trails, absence of sharp corners, and moderate steepness of hills make this an ideal area at which to start. Besides being competent teachers, the instructors are engaging and patient so that the whole experience becomes neophyte-friendly. If you're more experienced, the excellent trail grooming sets you up to ski farther, or faster, or with more finesse. I cannot think of a calmer environment for learning to ski or for developing your skating skills without fear of being in anyone else's way.

Because this is a well-forested skiing area, the trees' wind sheltering is excellent. Yet the bark, twigs, and pollen powders that can be a nuisance in the early spring are minimal with trails this wide. Though the skiing mileage isn't great, the skating lane's smoothness between the two sets of tracks for striding is conducive to practicing the "Vee-one" skate. In this most advanced skating method you combine double poling with every foot movement. Besides requiring your being fit and well balanced, the grooming must be very smooth for the

V1 to be effective. I liked the place so well that I drove here three times from the Bay Area while researching this book.

One mile farther up the road from the Nordic Center is the base lodge of the Shasta Ski Park downhill skiing operation. Here, your proximity to Mt. Shasta is awe-inspiring. Use their lifts to go telemark skiing, the Nordic skier's most elegant way to ski downhill. You don't need heavy alpine equipment with this technique, but what light gear you do need the Nordic Center can rent you. They can also set you up with a telemark lesson on beginner or intermediate slopes.

## Where to stay and eat

There are many places to stay 5 miles east or west of the Nordic Ski Center's turnoff to Hwy. 89. Heading east, McCloud has several outstanding hotels but is short on good restaurants. I enjoyed Lee and Marilyn Ogden's hospitality at the **McCloud Hotel**, Bed and Breakfast, (800) 964-2823. It reminds me of a classic English country hotel, where good service and comfort are what you expect—and get. While breakfasts are Marilyn's special treat for her guests, the hotel also provides an excellent buffet supper. With 13 comfortable rooms and four suites the McCloud Hotel earns a four-star rating from *Best Inns of California*. Prices range from $74 to $148 for double occupancy. **Raymond's**

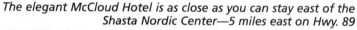

*The elegant McCloud Hotel is as close as you can stay east of the Shasta Nordic Center—5 miles east on Hwy. 89*

McCloud Hotel

33

*The inexpensive Finlandia Motel is as close as you can stay west of Shasta Nordic Center—5 miles west on Hwy. 89*

**Italian Ristorante**, the only sizable family restaurant in town, is nearby.

In and around Mt. Shasta I found two outstanding lodgings. The one in town, **Strawberry Valley Inn**, enjoys an excellent reputation, (530) 926-2052. Innkeeper Susie Ryan has done a wonderful job appointing the rooms and suites; the atmosphere warmly reflects her hospitality. Every evening in the reception lodge, the convivial *vin d'honeur* (a complementary glass of wine) for guests sets you up to go out for dinner. An extensive, self-service continental breakfast is included in the rates. Room rates range from $55 to $75 double occupancy.

Approaching Mt. Shasta on I-5 from the south, the first lodging you see as you exit the freeway is the **Finlandia Motel**, (530) 926-5596. Twelve years ago, after a cold night sleeping out at 11,000 feet on Mt. Shasta, climbing it on skis, I stayed here for $13. While costing more now, the Finlandia still offers the best group rates in the vicinity. Since owner Eila Rousseau comes from Finland, there's a Finnish family sauna available for guests. Three of the 23 units have kitchens, and the biggest unit has its own laundry. This unit with six beds for $75 per night has to be the best bargain I've come across anywhere. Prices range from a room for $35 per couple to the unit described at $75.

Mt. Shasta has a range of restaurant cuisines: American, French, Mexican, Italian, and Chinese. I found **Serge's** (French) for dinner and **Lily's** (American) for Sunday brunch to be the best. **Trinity** (American) has a good reputation, too.

Many other restaurants and lodgings are listed in the "Shasta Ski Board and Ski Park" brochure, obtainable by phone or Web site (see Area 1—At a Glance).

## A Full Weekend at Shasta

To make the most of my Shasta experience I not only put together two days' skiing, but also took advantage of the route leading to the great mountain, celebrating St. Valentine's Day in a unique way. But the several highlights I had in mind would make a memorable skiing weekend at any time during the ski season.

My traveling companion, Keatin, and I reached the Sacramento National Wildlife Refuge at Delevan on Friday by 4 P.M. to get the best of the afternoon light. This refuge borders Interstate 5. By taking the Princeton off-ramp (Road 68) east, we found ourselves at a wonderful complex of ponds and marshes, teeming with waterfowl. A $3 fee admitted us to the elevated, unpaved observation road winding several miles through the refuge. Already we could see great skeins of snow geese filling the sky. When these geese broke up their long flight formation and sideslipped in a rapid descent, they gabbled with such strident voices that their undertone of excitement was almost lost.

Besides the snow geese, two tundra swans, and twelve species of duck, within our allotted hour we see many northern harriers quartering the marshes and a mature bald eagle scanning a pond from a tree. Perhaps it's planning a duck dinner before dark. Then we see a much smaller predator, a northern shrike, whose menu includes mice, chickadees, and little warblers. Leaving the refuge, we hear a black-crowned night heron give a loud "kwark" and see two great horned owls fly from a thicket where they've hidden all day. Clearly, this wildlife refuge provides little respite from predators.

≈

We continue north beyond Redding and Shasta Lake until—just outside Mt. Shasta—we reach the Finlandia Motel. I like this motel, which reminds me of *Finlandia hiihto* (the ski race of Finland). That race winds 75 kms from Hameenlinna through forests and over frozen lakes to Lahti. Lahti is Mecca to all Finnish skiers, who turn out by the thousands to cheer racers crossing the finish line. I've skied this epic marathon twice and felt buoyed up by the huge crowd's encouragement,

*"Sisu, sisu"* (guts, guts), as we come striding out of the forest. You ski—totally wasted—downhill toward your goal through the applauding walls of spectators lining the curves, and their voices carry you across the line.

On Saturday after a day's skiing, we get ready to dine in elegant style aboard the **Shasta Sunset Dinner Train**, which will zigzag slowly uphill through the forest from McCloud to Mt. Shasta. At 6 P.M. it's snowing as we drive east to the old timber town of McCloud. The McCloud Railway Company's dinner train is stationed opposite the McCloud Hotel. McCloud Railway is owned and operated by Jeff and Verline Orbis, who are at the footrail of one of the cars greeting passengers, as snow falls like confetti all around us. Ladies are handed long-stemmed red roses as they board (it's St. Valentine's Day), and we are escorted to our tables for the round trip to Mt. Shasta. Of four classic cars from the 20s that make up the train, one is exclusively for entertainment and dancing.

The most impressive thing about this candlelight dinner may be the railroad car's interior. Its elegant restoration was a work of love and art. Verline tells us that the curtains and table settings were her refinements, but the entire Orbis family is involved—even the serving staff are related to our hosts. Cooking on the train is streamlined, with each guest's entree

*Mount Shasta presides over skiers crossing a meadow 9,000' below its summit*

Kevin Lahey

preselected when making reservations. While fish or fowl is the choice, tonight the fish is baked Alaska salmon and a filet mignon stands in for fowl.

As we journey slowly through the forest, we make three stops, switchbacking tracks to ascend the steep grade to Shasta. Two walls of dense pines, standing like sentinel rows in deep snowbeds, are illuminated by halogen lamps from the train. It has stopped snowing when I point down from our car to fresh deer tracks meandering the still corridor between train and trees. Train lovers and romantics are not mutually exclusive; if you're either or both of these, take this trip. Call (800) 733-2141 to make the necessary reservations.

≈

When I wrote a piece for the *San Francisco Chronicle*—"Outdoors" section—on getting started in cross-country skiing some years ago, I came to research it at Shasta, an outpost on the California Nordic scene. The skiing area seemed likely to be less populated than other areas farther south that I regularly skied. It was and is. And besides the Shasta Ski Park's well-run downhill and Nordic operations, the awe-inspiring mountain rises 9,000 feet above them, an island in the sky. The Shasta Sunset Dinner Train is a romantic opportunity with a good head of steam. If you choose to spend another night in the area, the Lower Klamath Wildlife Refuge is also in easy range on Highway 99. In winter months it's home to elegant tundra swans, snow geese, and more bald eagles than any other site in the United States. For its variety of events on a skiing weekend, Mt. Shasta greatly repays any effort to get there.
❅

# Area 2—At a Glance

### Eagle Mountain Resort Cross Country Skiing

Box 1566, Nevada City, CA 95959

phone (530) 389-2254          fax (530) 389-8033

www.eaglemtnresort.com

### Distance From

| | | |
|---|---|---|
| Bay Area—148 mi. | Stockton—85 mi. | Davis—72 mi. |
| Sacramento—65 mi. | Nevada City—22 mi. | Reno—64 mi. |

### Elevation, Facilities, & Hours

| | | |
|---|---|---|
| Trails—5,732-6,200' | Groomed—86 kms | Warming huts—2 |
| No dogs | Snowshoeing—all trails | Hours—9 A.M.-5 P.M. |

### Passes & Rental Prices

| | Adult (17-58) | Sr. (59+) | Jr. (12-16) |
|---|---|---|---|
| Trail pass | $16.50 | $10 | $8.50 |
| Skis, boots, poles | | | |
| track skis | $16.50 | - | - |
| skating skis | $18 | - | - |
| Snowshoes | $16.50 | - | - |
| Pulk sled | $20 | - | - |

### Ski School

Full package $36 for all-day trail pass, rentals, and lesson.

Group track or skating lesson $18.

Private lesson $25.

**Snow Play Area:** for children and pulk sleds for use on groomed trails.

### Lodging & Food

Rainbow Lodge, (530) 426-3871, is 6 mi. east on I-80. Colfax (26 mi.) and Auburn are just west, with many hotel and food options. Nevada City's Outside Inn (22 mi. west) is recommended, (530) 265-2233. The Shang Garden Restaurant in Colfax serves good Chinese cuisine; there are many good restaurants in Nevada City. Eagle Mountain Cross-country Lodge has hot drinks and food.

**Summer Program:** The resort becomes a mountain-bike park, with tent-cabins and camping; it's also the site for The Wilderness Institute's Leadership and Team Building Program.

# 6 Central California
# Eagle Mountain

## AREA 2. EAGLE MOUNTAIN RESORT
## CROSS COUNTRY SKIING
### (Closest Cross-country Ski Resort to the Bay Area)

### Summary

Because Eagle Mountain Resort is at a low elevation (under 6,000') skiing may start later than in the 7,000-foot areas. But offering by far the least highway hassle during frequent winter storms is its great advantage. The proximity to Sacramento (a 1-hour drive), Auburn, and Nevada City makes it a favorite for day trips. Eagle Mountain maintains 86 kms of well-groomed trails for track skiing and skating through rolling wooded country. The comfortable base lodge has all amenities. With lessons, tours, weekend races, barbecues, and full-moon night skiing available, the program is both thorough and intriguing.

### How to get there

Eagle Mountain Resort is 26 miles east of Colfax near I-80. *From cities east or west*, use I-80 and exit at Yuba Gap. Go south on Lake Valley Rd., bearing right at the large SNOW PARK sign. Directed by the red-and-yellow EAGLE MOUNTAIN CROSS-COUNTRY sign, go 1 mile and turn left into a spacious parking lot. The lodge is at the back of the lot. *From Nevada City* take Hwy. 20 east toward Truckee. At the junction with I-80 in 22 miles, head 0.25 mile west to the Yuba Gap exit. Continue as described above.

## Description of skiing area

Eagle Mountain's cross-country skiing trails are located in a wooded area with numerous meadows and lakes in the Sierra foothills. The resort is bounded by I-80 to the north and the North Fork of the American River to the south (neither of which you see or hear). The 86 kms of trails are well groomed, with a skating lane between twin tracks set for striding. The low-elevation trails have a variable hilly terrain but nothing very steep. The well-built, rustic wooden lodge is comfortable and spacious inside. Everything you need except the bathrooms—they're in a separate building—is in this lodge: trail pass, equipment rentals, class sign-up, plus food and drinks. A large, elevated sundeck is ideal for picnicking or just hanging out.

Dylan Gradhandt and his lodge staff, ski instructors, and first-aid ski patrol, are friendly and helpful. (If you break a piece of your own equipment, they'll try to mend it before renting you a replacement—I like that.) Two bonuses at this area are the $10 full-day pass for anyone over 59 years old, and the 30 minutes you're allowed to ski on the trails to test conditions. You get a rain check and a free cup of coffee if you're not happy with them.

If you want a weekend's skiing without committing yourself to the longer Lake Tahoe Region drive, this may be the place for you. But be sure to check first on the snowpack at Eagle Mountain; it's less than you'll find 12 miles east and another 1,000 feet up the road. While early season snow can look fine, there has to be a deep enough snow base before the grooming machines can be put effectively to work.

## Where to stay and eat

The best lodging is only 6 miles east of Eagle Mountain at the Rainbow exit of I-80. **Rainbow Lodge** has prices ranging from $89 to $139 for a family suite, (530) 426-3661. **The Engadine Cafe** in the lodge provides outstanding gourmet meals. At the Soda Springs-Norden exit, another 6 miles east, you'll find a 24-hour gas station open year-round. A good motel 22 miles west of Eagle Mountain in Nevada City is **The Outside Inn** (www.outsideinn.com). Owned by hard-core kayaker Evans Phelps, the motel caters particularly to outdoors enthusiasts with rooms for $55 or a suite for $85, and has won awards for its courtyard design.

The **Colfax Motor Lodge** 26 miles west of Eagle Mountain has rooms for $29.95, (530) 346-8382. I've bailed out there many times on my way to Donner during snowstorms. **Rosy's Cafe** is a good American diner next to this motel. On the south side of I-80 at Colfax (on South Canyon Way), there's good Chinese cuisine—Szechwan, Mandarin, or Hunan—at **Shang Garden Restaurant**.

Daphne Hougard

*Eagle Mountain Ski Lodge is only 65 miles east of Sacramento on I-80*

## *Citizen Racing at Eagle Mountain*

Whether you're a road runner or either a cross-country runner or skier, "citizen racing" lets people at any level of proficiency participate. Anyone can compete within their peer gender, age, or special-circumstance group. For instance, with a guide, totally blind cross-country skiers can compete in the same events as people with no handicap. Later I'll describe how athletes unable to walk take part in long-distance, cross-country ski races. In citizen racing everyone gets the chance to compare their equipment and test their skill, stamina, and conditioning without the stress of having to meet a particular standard. You don't have to win the race to feel good; you feel good because you did your best. And that's your prize.

To become a better skier you either take lessons or ski with friends willing and able to coach you. Improving your skills and fitness this way may be enough for you. However, when you become more proficient, you may want to become a volunteer ski patroller, a racer—or both. I met Leslie Thompson, aged 52, of Nevada City last winter, who had recently learned to ski, got her first-aid certificate, and was then ski patrolling at Eagle Mountain. (Leslie is in the background of the photo showing little Katelin skiing with her parents.) Leslie told me she was going to try her first race—a 10-km, classical-style one—the coming Saturday. I suggested we go skiing together and soon we were sharing a diagonal-stride clinic in preparation for Saturday.

I've been off the snow for several years, after a long competitive racing career in Europe, Canada, New England, and California. While I love racing, in recent years it's all been ocean-kayaking events for me. Here was my chance to race on skis again and I couldn't resist it. I told Leslie that I'd probably start in the race myself, and I meant only *start* because racing 10 kms at 6,000 feet when you've done nothing like it for five years is a tall order. But if you want to do something out of the ordinary, at least start!

On Saturday Leslie and I were both there. So, too, were a number of the best racers in the Masters age groups from the Lake Tahoe Region. Helga Sable, many times a US national champion, from Kings Beach, was there with her husband Art, an old rival of mine. Philip Molard from Squaw Valley, another national champion, was there. Dan Hill, the Fischer rep from Truckee, was there. From Mammoth Lakes, Barbara Cameron, another good racer, was present. Then there were several members of **Paco's Bike and Ski Shop**'s racing team, sharp in their club racing suits and fast on their skis. Since I'd raced with all these people many times over the years, it was like old times. And it was great to see them looking older but fit as ever.

*Dad pulls the pulk (sled) while Mom follows Katelin, who needs no poles at 3 years old*

Everyone is busy waxing their skis for the race—the consensus being that either a hard purple wax or a violet klister (with the consistency of glue) will work well on the tracks. Some skiers prepare two pairs of skis to try out both waxes before deciding which to race on. Helga Sable calls out to me, "Hey, Mike, the women want to have their own start! Can't you do something about it?" She's seen I've been spending time talking with Tai Boutell, who's going to start the race. And I do suggest to Tai that this is the fairest way to start. "Sure," he agrees, "we'll give them a 2-minute head start."

When you have outstanding women skiers lined up with the men in a mass start on skis, they have an immediate disadvantage. At the start of the race, some men who neither ski as well nor as fast over the long haul as these women will double-pole to the front, using their arm strength. Since there is limited space on the groomed trail, these men block the track early in the race. It's frustrating for the women.

At 31° the snow conditions and the air temperature are both perfect. The race starts and off the women go—a bevy of brave hearts scurrying over the snow like quail. The men start 2 minutes later. It's a small field of about 40 dedicated skiers; and since I have photos to take of both starts, I lose a few minutes before I get going. Although my violet klister is working well and I'm skiing smoothly, I soon feel the strain. For Heaven's sake, I've had the flu for two weeks, haven't skied for five years, and am 65 years old pretending I'm 45.

Cowbells are ringing as volunteers marking the course swing them to and fro to encourage the skiers. This is California so the air temperature has already risen a few degrees since we started, but my wax is holding well because most of the track is under tree cover where snow stays cool. While track grooming is good and skiing conditions are perfect, my own condition isn't. The 5-km loop course is to be skied twice, and by the time we reach the meadow from which we started I've caught and passed two of the slower skiers. But now I have to pull up.

I've skied that 5-km (3.2-mile) loop as fast as possible and my chest is hurting. To go farther in my state would be foolish, so I retrieve my camera and take shots of the fit skiers as they finish. Not surprisingly, Dan Hill wins the race, while Leslie Thompson, whose first race this was, finishes well last. Yet, though Leslie comes in last she's pleased, as she should be.

❋

## Areas 3 & 4—At a Glance

### Royal Gorge Cross Country Ski Resort
### including Wilderness & Rainbow lodges
Box 1100, Soda Springs, CA 95728
(800) 500-3871      for local calls (530) 426-3871
fax (530) 426-9221      www.royalgorge.com

### Distance From
Los Angeles—400 mi.    Fresno—300 mi.        San Jose—250 mi.
Bay Area—185 mi.       Sacramento—85 mi.     Reno—54 mi.

### Nearest Airport
Reno—54 miles (serving all national airlines)

### Light Aircraft
Truckee-Tahoe Airport—14 miles (non-commercial)

### Elevation, Facilities, & Hours
Trails—6,700-8,000'       Groomed—328 kms       Telemark—4 lifts
Warming huts—10          Snowshoeing—all trails
Dogs—Van Norden only     Hours—8:30 A.M.-5 P.M. weekends
                         9 A.M.-5 P.M. midweek

### Passes & Rental Prices (free trail pass for children 12-)

|  | Adult (18-59) | Jr. (13-17) | Child (Under 12) |
|---|---|---|---|
| Trail pass | $21.50 | $8.50 | - |
| Skis, boots, poles track/skating skis | $17.50 | - | - |
| Snowshoes | $16 | - | - |
| Pulk sled | $15 | - | - |

### Ski School

|  | Adult (18-59) | Jr. (13-17) | Child (Under 12) |
|---|---|---|---|
| Trail pass & lesson | $34 | - | - |
| Trail pass, lesson & equipment | $42 | $25 | - |

**Pee Wee Snow School:** Weekends & Peak Season $45 all day; $30 A.M., $20 P.M.

### Lodging & Food
Royal Gorge's Rainbow Lodge and The Engadine Cafe are 7 miles west on I-80 at the Rainbow exit, (503) 426-3871.

### Wilderness Lodge Rates
Includes three full meals per day, showers, hot tub, trail passes, lessons, and guided tours. Private room rates are per person, double occupancy, with a variety of room designs: Weekend (2-day), adult $129-$169; child (5-16) $85-$125. Private cabins with full Wilderness Lodge program $229.

### Rainbow Lodge
7 miles west of Soda Springs on I-80. Terminus of Interconnect Ski Trail.

# 7    TAHOE REGION
# SodA Springs

## AREA 3. ROYAL GORGE CROSS COUNTRY SKI RESORT

### Summary

Royal Gorge is the most comprehensive Nordic skiing resort in North America. The groomed trails stretch web-like from Sugar Bowl Ski Area, across Lake Van Norden Meadow, through forests mantling Devil's Peak and beyond. You can stay at Sugar Bowl Lodge and ski more than a 100 miles to reach Royal Gorge's Rainbow Lodge, only 15 miles away as the raven flies, if you want to ski a really long route to get there. Or stay at Rainbow Lodge and take the shuttle bus to Summit Station, ski all day, and be bussed back. On weekends there are four lifts to help you practice your telemark turns, or get you on your way home. And kids under 12 ski for free!

### How to get there

*From the Bay Area* Royal Gorge Summit Station is a 3.5-hour drive, 185 miles east on I-80. Exit at Soda Springs-Norden, where there's a 76 Gas Station open 24 hours every day. This facility is less than 2 miles from the ski resort. Heading east, turn right off the ramp and go 0.6 mile on Donner Pass Rd. to the junction with Soda Springs Rd. Turn right and follow the signs to Royal Gorge Summit Station. *From Reno* take I-80 west for 54 miles to the Soda Springs-Norden exit. Continue as above.

## Description of skiing area

An extensive network of five interconnected track systems was designed by John Slouber, the owner/operator of this magnificent skiing area. When snow conditions permit and the complete track system is open, there are 328 kms of varied skiing over mountain, lake-basin, and forest terrain. Over 200 miles of trails thread 9,000 wilderness acres, requiring the largest fleet of snow grooming machines at any cross-country ski area with groomed trails. Royal Gorge can offer—most years in this heavy snowbelt—five full months of skiing.

The operation is composed of track systems—each covering a large area—where you can explore many interconnected trails, starting from and returning to your chosen base. The **Van Norden Track System** offers miles of easy, flat skiing between Sugar Bowl and Soda Springs, with intermittent warming huts to make a cup of tea or heat up some soup. Van Norden has its own ticket booth (tickets accessing all track systems) and parking lot, located just after you cross the railroad tracks on the Soda Springs Rd. It has acquired its own identity as the Van Norden Cross Country Ski Area.

Along the perimeters of Van Norden you can ski undulating trails lined by tall pines and one steep ascent, which has a kinder slope for your descent. From this system you can ski into the **Summit Track System** by crossing Soda Springs Rd. (take your skis off to do this) and skiing a short distance up to Summit Station. Or by making a big sweep south, you can access the **Ice Lakes Track System** without crossing any road. Route combinations are legion; they could fill a whole week's ski touring without repeating any trail.

*Two parents pull their infants Norwegian-style, setting out from Summit Station*

Daphne Hougard

At **Summit Station,** where most people start their day, you'll find the Royal Gorge headquarters and all ancillary services. They have the largest selection of rental equipment here—all of it Fischer and Salomon—and much of it designed by John Slouber for Royal Gorge. A ski shop sells a full line of ski clothing, gloves, sunblock, and sunglasses. (Remember to wear shades and sunblock when skiing or suffer consequences.) A restaurant, a spacious sundeck, and an upstairs bar make the Summit Station a pleasant base or rendezvous with friends.

Royal Gorge's red shuttle bus operates daily between Summit Station and Rainbow Lodge (weather permitting) and connects on weekends with Sugar Bowl and lodges along Donner Pass Rd. Here's your chance to start out from Sugar Bowl Ski Area and ski back to Summit Station. (You may not leave a car at Sugar Bowl's parking lot unless you are staying there or purchasing their pass.)

With the Summit Station at 7,000 feet as your base, you can ski south, gradually ascending the **Palisade Peak Track System** for a view of the real Royal Gorge, from which the ski resort takes its name. It is a dramatic 4,417 feet deep. Or stay close to the Summit Station and use any of the short 4-to-6-km trails that take you downhill to **Wilderness Lodge** at 6,700 feet. Here you can take a break; climb the outside stairs to the cafe sundeck and enjoy tea, coffee, soup, chili, pastries, and cool drinks. From here you can decide your next move. All of the trails are 20 feet wide and prepared for track skiing and skating. While snowshoers may use any trail, they should walk on the trail margins. (This is for your safety. Skiers traveling faster than you cannot stop or step aside as easily as you can.)

Fitter and expert skiers, most of whom are racers, like to ski many miles and ski them fast. Some ski 50 kms (over 30 miles) before lunch. Although they have an almost endless trail network here, most racers come by Wilderness Lodge at some point on their route. If you watch them ski you see the technical standard a fit person can attain; by taking clinics and putting in the miles you can, too. If you're a competent skier and a bit of a peregrine, albeit not a racer, you can point your skis from Wilderness Lodge toward the **Devils Peak Track System.** While there's a warming hut out there, it's a long way back to Summit Station; so watch the time and ski this area with a friend.

Finally, there's the **Rainbow Interconnect Trail,** which takes you down, down, downhill to **Rainbow Lodge** on I-80. It's open only on weekends toward the end of the season when there's abundant snow. Don't do it unless you're competent and fit. After climbing steeply toward the Devil's Peak, the Interconnect peels off—right—from the Wagon Train Trail. A big sign and a black-diamond grading mark the start of the route. A "one-way only" trail of some charm until you close on the crux of it, its charm rapidly resolves into a downhill challenge. Narrow, tightly cornered, and seriously steep! When you reach Rainbow Lodge, go straight to the bar to claim your reward. When the Interconnect Trail is open, shuttle-bus service is available from Rainbow Lodge back to Summit Station.

Royal Gorge

*Mass start at Royal Gorge's 50-km California Gold Rush*

## The California Gold Rush

The Great American Ski Chase, a series of marathon races held annually across the nation, stages its last race at Royal Gorge. It's a 50-km event with a prize of one ounce of gold and a national title for the winner in each age group. In conjunction with this event there is also the Silver Rush, a race of 25 or 30 kms, depending on what's at stake. The 1999 US Women's 30-Km National Championship was held in conjunction with the Silver Rush, so the distance for the Silver Rush prize was increased to 30 kms. A new race, the Bronze Rush for Juniors, was added to the skiing festival that year.

## Pricing

Trail pass prices are higher at Royal Gorge than at any other California area. They have to be. Royal Gorge features more miles of grooming and a huge fleet of machines with highly skilled drivers to do it; and there are more facilities, including four lifts, with a bigger staff than at any cross-country ski resort in North America. An upscale outfit, Royal Gorge is not run economy class. Despite this, there are many good discounts, ranging from the Season Pass, the 10-Day Pass, Age Discounts, and—most helpful of all to parents—a Free Pass for kids under 12.

## Where to stay above snowline

In the immediate vicinity of Royal Gorge your lodging options are numerous, and some are remarkably inexpensive. In Soda Springs and adjacent Serene Lakes areas near Royal Gorge, there are many houses and condos managed by

**Castle Realty Vacation Rentals**, (530) 426-1226. The most economic lodging bunks you dormitory-style using your own sleeping bag and is 3 miles east at Norden on Donner Pass Rd., **Clair Tappaan Lodge**, (530) 426-3632. With its 150 beds, many people can stay here while skiing at Royal Gorge for $37 each, which includes two hot meals and a bag lunch. Farther up Donner Pass Rd., another bunkhouse bargain with 70 beds and 5 private rooms is the $25 bed and breakfast at **Alpine Skills International's Donner Spitz Hutte**, (530) 426-9108.

Royal Gorge's own **Rainbow Lodge** is 7 miles west on I-80 at the Rainbow Rd. exit, (530) 426-3871. This warm, old stone-and-timber building has very comfortable public and private rooms, plus two dining rooms. Thirty-one rooms and suites range in price from $79 to $139. With an engagingly rustic atmosphere and its unique collection of early 20th century European skiing posters, this hotel is your best bet.

## Staying below the deep snowline

The **Truckee Hotel**, in "Old Town" Truckee, (530) 587-4444, is a charming but train-noisy hotel with a good dining room. Its 37 rooms have prices for double occupancy ranging from $45 to $125. The **Best Western Hotel**, just southeast of Truckee on Hwy. 267, is a large, modern hotel with 100 rooms and suites, ranging in price from $88 to $169. I've stayed here and found it both comfortable and quiet. Because it's only 0.5 mile from the Truckee-Tahoe Airport, people flying in to ski at Royal Gorge often stay here. Coming east to Soda Springs on I-80 at night during heavy winter storms, often I've bailed out for $30 at the **Colfax Motor Lodge**, (530) 346-8382.

## Where to eat

The **Engadine Cafe**, the smaller of two dining rooms in Rainbow Lodge, is excellent. Don't be misled. "Cafe" is both a French and Swiss idiom for many a fine restaurant and the Engadine Cafe qualifies. The French and California cuisines for breakfast, brunch, lunch, and dinner are superb. Both the **Passage Restaurant** in the Truckee Hotel and the **Cottonwood Restaurant** at Hilltop Lodge, which overlooks the Truckee River as you head southeast of town on Hwy. 267, are good. If you've never eaten a baked cottontail and would like to, it's on the Cottonwood menu. For the budget-conscious—with kids—there's a **Sizzler** in Truckee, in the shopping center where Donner Pass Rd. meets Hwy. 89 south for Squaw Valley.

## *One Way Only to Rainbow Lodge*

Of all the routes you can ski at Royal Gorge one of the best and probably the most challenging is from Sugar Bowl Ski Resort via Royal Gorge Summit Station to Rainbow Lodge on I-80. This route has a good Nordic feel to it because you are skiing in essence from one homestead to another; it's a 30-km shuttle trip rather than a loop. On your Royal Gorge map the route takes you from the top left (east) corner to the bottom right (west) corner. If you don't want to ski that far, start from Summit Station and ski 22 kms down to Rainbow Lodge. This cuts out 8 kms and omits the Sugar Bowl shuttle for your start. The last 8 kms of the Rainbow Interconnect Trail add hot curry to your rice course.

Friends who ski the Royal Gorge track systems consistently have been telling me for years about a new trail called Rainbow Interconnect. This winter, returning to the slopes after several seasons away, I was often asked, "Have you skied it yet?" The unique character of this new route is its steepness, so steep that a number of determined skiers among my friends have been intimidated by it. When the snowpack was deep enough, at the end of February 1999, I decided to ski the new route. Yet, cautious after my long break from skiing, I put on lightweight backcountry skis with metal edges that I thought would help get me safely down the steep stuff—my trusty Fischer E 99s.

Leaving Summit Station I bumped into Royal Gorge proprietor and designer John Slouber and asked him, "Is the Rainbow Trail as difficult as I keep hearing?" He smiled and said, "After you cross the railroad tracks it gets steep." So I said, "How steep?" And all John did was grimace, while shaking his wrists like Marcel Marceau miming anguish. Off I went, pondering this nonverbal critique.

On my backcountry Fischers with the crown-base configuration under the midsection for grip, I wasn't in any hurry. If you learn the diagonal stride on racing skis, you'll find the same efficient body movements and skiing techniques serve you well on any skis. Using good form without hurrying, I tackled the 22 kms ahead.

Taking the Palisade Trail to the top of Lift 4, I put in a few telemark turns to the bottom of the piste and continue on Palisade to Stage Coach Trail. I follow Stage Coach around Deer Lake to pick up Wiesel, passing the huge boulder called "Big Rock" on my way to the Upper Cascade Warming Hut. This popular resting place is about as far as some touring skiers go, if they've started from Summit Station. I stop near the hut to drink my Gatorade, rather than make tea inside as I sometimes do. One of two people leaving the hut asks me, "Are you

*With Castle Peak in the background, two skiers approach their picnic spot on the Rainbow Interconnect Trail*

skiing to Rainbow Lodge?" When I say, "Yes," the other person exclaims, "Oh my!" and asks, "Have you done it before?" I ask them how much farther it is, and when told it's 15 kms I realize the need to get going. With afternoon drawing on, my final commitment to do the route must be made. Oh yes, I have thought of making tea in the hut, wasting some time, and then telling myself it's too late to complete it.

In the next 4 kms I slog several hundred feet up Wagon Train to reach 7,300 feet. That the crown base of my E 99s allows me to walk up all the steep sections over soft snow without having to herringbone is the good news. Yet, I still use a lot of arm strength and know-how to do it. Next, a trail junction unexpectedly leading right bears a large sign: ONE WAY ONLY—8 KMS—TO RAINBOW LODGE. Great! The people who said I had 15 to go were off by 3 kms, so I'm in good shape.

Onward and downward. I am skiing easily, slightly downhill. The snow is so soft by 3 P.M. that it's better suited to striding than skating. As I move along, two people come into view ahead and we're soon sharing the track. After skiing round a bend, a break in the forest before us allows a fine view north to Castle Peak. On a small plateau Lucien and Ellen stop to rest and I snap a few photos of them before I ski on.

I no sooner wonder where's the steepness is before I get my first taste. I round a bend to find a young woman already set up in a strong snowplow for a steep downhill curve over open ground. Passing, I discover why she's already set up her snowplow. The curve tightens into a sickle, swinging out of view into the forest. As I enter the shade of trees the snow completely changes; it goes dead, cloying like wet blotting paper. I drop into a low telemark kneel just in time to avoid a face-plant.

Two fit-looking young women on skating skis wait at the end of this downhill. They ask me if I've seen their friend. I tell them she's coming down safely and ask, "Is that the steep stuff I've heard about?" They both laugh, and one says, "If that's steep you're in for a surprise—that's nothing." As I ski away I hear the other ask, "Did you see his skis?"

A few short climbs and easy descents later I'm at the railroad tracks. Off with my skis, down a snowbank, cross the tracks, and up the snowbank onto the trail again. While there's some steep climbing, there's much steeper ground ahead. As I crest the last climb I hear the tractor-trailers roaring down below on I-80.

If you drive past Rainbow Lodge on the freeway, you can accurately judge the steep escarpment rising behind the North Fork of the American River. And that river cascades right beside Rainbow Lodge. I've looked up many times from my truck and wondered how in hell anyone could make a skiing route out of it. Now I find out.

Well, it is steep—very steep—and the trail is narrow. But, unlike a route I once skied in Austria, it's not terrifying. When Lee Norris and I telemarked the Giant Slalom Course at St. Anton in 1975, we were on the original E 99s, the old green ones. Mine were 215 centimeters long and Lee's were 205s. She led the way down, switching between parallel skiing and telemarking. The course we were skiing had been used only the week before for the World Cup. That descent is my reference point for vertical terror on cross-country skis. I fell three times, while Lee, an elite alpine ski racer and instructor at both Obergurgle in Austria and Mad River Glen in Vermont, smoked it.

With the narrow trail falling away before me, my mind flashed also on *Coureurs de Bois*, the 100-mile marathon in Canada where some Laurentian downhill trails are horrendously fast. On the Rainbow Interconnect the difficulty isn't steepness; the narrowness of the trail—tightness of the turns—leave no room to run out from a mistake. With my E 99s on soft, late-afternoon snow it's a challenge but not an extreme one. Rainbow Interconnect definitely has character and a deserved reputation, but a competent skier can complete it. So down I go, with a mixed bag of stem turns, telemarks, a few sideslips, and a little panache.

To let others know who might want to try it, I had timed myself. Skiing with one break, the 22 kms (13.75 miles) took me 3.5 hours. Now that I knew the trail I wanted to ski it again on faster skis. The following morning on my Fischer racing skis I skated the route without at any time trying to ski fast. It was a cooler day, so I set off at 11 A.M. to catch the firmness of the track and the good glide that goes with it. I anticipated a slightly softer track later that would help me when I reached the steep downhill section. In 1 hour, 35 minutes, I was at Rainbow Lodge, to catch the shuttle bus back up to Summit Station. ❄

## For skiing the Sugar Bowl-Rainbow Lodge Interconnect Trail

**1.** Don't leave a car at the Sugar Bowl parking lot unless you are staying there or have purchased a lift ticket for that day.
**2.** Stay at Rainbow Lodge and take the Royal Gorge shuttle bus to Sugar Bowl, and ski back to Rainbow Lodge (an ideal way to go).
**3.** Park at Royal Gorge Summit Station, shuttle to Sugar Bowl, ski back to your car, or continue all the way to Rainbow Lodge and shuttle back to your car.
**4.** Don't enter any of the Royal Gorge track systems without that day's pass.

# AREA 4. ROYAL GORGE WILDERNESS LODGE

## Summary

This is an exclusive lodge: there are no interruptions in the continuum of good food, skiing instruction and free skiing, hot tubs, comfortable beds, and pleasant company. With no telephone poles in sight there's no transportation to Wilderness Lodge other than its sleigh. From this sanctuary a good 5 kms from Summit Station, you can ski the whole Royal Gorge Track System. The ski guides are also your hosts in the lodge; they are a cheerful crew who hail from far corners of the globe—Vermont, Alaska, Australia, England, France, and South Africa this year. They take good care of you.

## How to get there

Follow the routes to Royal Gorge Summit Station in "How to get there" for Area 3, and be sure to park your car and assemble your gear at the designated time

*At Wilderness Lodge meals are excellent, wine is complimentary, and the company is good*

David Madison/Royal Gorge

and place here. The only way to Wilderness Lodge as a guest is via the 5-km sleigh ride, carrying you and all your gear, which leaves from Summit Station at dusk. Wrapped in fur robes, snugly protected from the early evening chill, you feel as if you're on your way to meet Dr. Zhivago.

## Description of program

This whole experience has to be smoothly scripted or it would unravel. Once you're on the sleigh you'll have no mundane concerns for the duration of your stay. On reaching your destination you'll find a new timber lodge that's full of character. All bunk cabins and bedrooms have comfortable beds with warm duvets. Bathroom facilities are communal: one for women, one for men, and one coed. The dining room downstairs has long tables where you sit and eat with

David Madison/Royal Gorge

*Guests travel warmly wrapped the 5 kms to the lodge*

fellow lodge guests, who all have at least two things in common—everyone's come to ski and everyone's left another life piling up in a mailbox.

Your package includes: all your meals (including wine available at lunch and dinner); all snacks (tea, coffee, hot chocolate, and lemonade); daily trail passes, lessons, and tours; hot tub and sauna; pre-breakfast stretching sessions led by a ski guide (for those who choose to participate); and video critiques of your day's skiing, in the evening. Lounge areas are spacious and well appointed, with classical music unobtrusively piped from somewhere. There are delicious appetizers before dinner. The meals are hearty and well prepared, with a vegetarian entree always available at dinner.

Since you'll need a few things the lodge can't supply, use a checklist when you pack. Clearly mark your gear so that you can retrieve it from the lobby on arrival. Wear warm boots and clothing for the 30-40-minute open sleigh ride, and bring a waterproof jacket (snow protection) for skiing. In the lodge you'll want some comfortable, casual clothes, and soft footwear. While you'll want your toiletries, hair blowers aren't needed here. Because skiing conditions often invite thin, layered rather than weatherproof clothing, lightweight ski pants, running tights, sweatpants, T-shirts, and long-sleeved shirts are all appropriate. With several light layers, you can put on and peel off garments that aren't a problem to carry. Besides a small pack for day trips, you'll need a hat, gloves, sunscreen, sunglasses, a camera, and plenty of film. You may also want a swimsuit for the hot tub and sauna and a light robe for trips to the bathroom and sauna.

John Stoddart, chief guide and lodge manager, coaches a guest downhill

David Madison/Royal Gorge

Any skiing equipment or snowshoes that you need or want to try out can be rented at Wilderness Lodge. The ski guides will advise you daily on waxing variables and help you plan your skiing time. You can choose to free ski for the duration of your stay; some experienced skiers do. However, a wide range of lessons are available—two per day—covering all techniques of cross-country skiing. These lessons not only benefit your skiing, they invite interaction with other guests and they're fun.

When it's time to leave Wilderness Lodge you may either ski out or ride back on the sleigh, now in full daylight. Either way, the sleigh will take your gear up to Summit Lodge. For all you get, the cost of the package is very reasonable. A price breakdown is included on "Areas 3 & 4—At a Glance" (see page 44), and all inquiries should be directed to the office, (800) 500-3871, or (530) 426-3871 locally.

## *The Complete Resort*

I didn't want to take the sleigh down to Wilderness Lodge because I'm a skier—I like to ski. But then John and Lynda Stoddart who manage the lodge would say, "That's part of the experience, mate. You're writing about what we have to offer." I've known these two Aussies since they showed up in Soda Springs some 20 years ago, so I put my skis in the sleigh's ski rack, bundled myself in furs, and sleighed away. Darkness was closing in on dusk as we set off from Summit Station. Flickering above breaks in the closely packed pines, the candles were all lit. I began to relax, letting go of my everyday concerns; it was quite lovely.

What a remarkable ski area John Slouber has designed at Royal Gorge. In the skiing industry the bigger your project *on the snow*, the more there is that can go wrong. I used to hear detractors say, "It's too big." "It won't work; not enough people are that interested." Twenty years later, Royal Gorge has more acres, more miles of trails for skiers to enjoy, and more variety of options than can be found at a privately owned resort anywhere in the world. A good motto for Royal Gorge Resort with its Summit Station, Wilderness Lodge, and Rainbow Lodge—its Lake Van Norden Meadow and 9,000 acres of skiing terrain would be: "More is more," rather than "Less is more." It was Aristotle who propounded that lesser line, and he wasn't talking about frugality.

About the time I came to California, in 1978, John Slouber and Jonathan Wiesel were developing their Nordic program at Soda Springs. A little man carrying his skis over one shoulder and smoking a big briar pipe was their logo. I could imagine him eating sauerkraut and wanting apple strudel for desert. In the late 70s that comfortably pedestrian image, a *langlaufer* carrying his skis—not on them—was appropriate enough. Who among us experiencing the start-up of the Royal Gorge operation could have imagined how the sport would grow in the next 20 years? John Slouber is one who did; this year he had over 100,000 day-visiting skiers in five months at "The Gorge." ❄

# Area 5—At a Glance

## Clair Tappaan Lodge & Hutchinson Lodge

Clair Tappaan Lodge, Box 36, Norden, CA 95724
phone (530) 426-3632    fax (530) 426-0742    www.sierraclub.org

### Distance From

| | | |
|---|---|---|
| Los Angeles—402.5 mi. | Fresno—302.5 mi. | San Jose—252.5 mi. |
| Bay Area—187.5 mi. | Sacramento—87.5 mi. | Reno—56.5 mi. |

### Elevation & Facilities

Trails—7,000-7,600'    Groomed—12 kms    Wilderness huts—4
No dogs    Unlimited miles of off-track ski touring and snowshoeing

## Bus Service

Sierra Club bus charters from as far as Orange County (check with manager); also regular bus schedule, year-round, to Soda Springs from Sacramento and Bay Area.

## Passes & Rental Prices (Day Visitors)

| | Adult | Child (under 12) |
|---|---|---|
| Trail pass | $7 | $3.50 |

| | First day | Each additional day |
|---|---|---|
| Backcountry skis | $16 | $14 |
| Track/skating skis | $14 | $11 |
| Snowshoes | $11 | - |

### Ski School

1-2 hours (depending on class size) $14.

### Lodging Prices

$41 for adults; $22-$26 (midweek and weekend) for children under 12; non-members add $5 per day. Includes two hot meals and one bag lunch per day. All guests do one house chore per day. Full day's use of groomed trails is free for lodge guests.

### Destination Lodging

140-bed dormitory bunk rooms; bring a sleeping bag.

### Alternate Lodging

For snow emergencies in Colfax, Auburn, & Nevada City (see "Where to stay and eat" [Chap. 6], page 40).

### Hutchinson Lodge

Next door to, and managed by, CTL, sharing the same track system. It is rented to approved groups and has basic facilities for guests to run their own program. Call (530) 426-3632.

# 8   Tahoe Region
# Norden to Donner Pass

## AREA 5. CLAIR TAPPAAN LODGE —SIERRA CLUB

### Summary

Clair Tappaan Lodge (CTL), built in 1934 by Sierra Club members, offers full board and bunk for up to 140 people throughout the ski season. It is run like a hostel-cooperative in which all guests contribute toward daily upkeep of the lodge by doing one specific chore. (There's a list of 80 chores to choose from.) With a good, hot breakfast and outstanding dinner, a self-prepared bag lunch, and no charge to ski the groomed trails, CTL provides the least expensive ski weekend. Other benefits include weekend folk dancing led by Bay Area expert Hal Rohlfing, a quiet, well-stocked reading room, and a hot tub for eight at a time. Clair Tappaan is close to the Boreal and Donner Ski Ranch lifts and 3 miles from Royal Gorge. Non-club members pay a small surcharge. Such a value may surprise you how far a dollar still goes; it's a unique family experience.

### How to get there

*From Sacramento or Reno*, exit from I-80 at Soda Springs-Norden. Drive 2.5 miles east on Donner Pass Rd. (Old Route 40) and look for the CTL sign on the left side of road. There is no driveway; the lodge is up a steep path with limited parking in front of the sign. The main parking lot is on your right at roadside beyond the lodge.

## Description of area

From the back door of Clair Tappaan Lodge you ski directly onto the ski school area. A groomed forest trail, Main Drag, leads steeply uphill from there, wending its way 2 miles east to Donner Ski Ranch. Yet, only 0.25 mile from CTL on Main Drag, the Ski Ranch downhill operation has a lift (Chair 3), giving lodge guests fast access to extensive, lift-served telemark territory. Boreal Ski Area, fronting I-80 to the north, has a lift ascending from Lytton Lake, a much-used snow meadow on the Main Drag trail to Donner Ski Ranch. This lift takes you to the summit of Boreal Ridge for a commanding view of Castle Peak, and provides access to Boreal Ski Area's main lodge.

Clair Tappaan's 12 kms of groomed trails offer convenient links to many miles of backcountry skiing. One particular route, which makes an excellent, intermediate day trip, follows Main Drag from the lodge, ascends Boreal Ridge, and easily descends a long, groomed trail down to I-80. After taking off your skis to walk under the freeway, you continue 5 kms on ungroomed snow to the Sierra Club's Peter Grubb Hut. This hut is in a beautiful location, a broad open basin surrounded by high mountains, with 9,000-foot Castle Peak dominant to the east. You can sleep overnight at this primitive hut (there are bunks and a fireplace), but it's booked for groups on weekends throughout the ski season, so check with CTL management first. (It can, of course, be used as an emergency shelter.)

A more advanced day trip from Clair Tappaan Lodge is via the groomed trails to Donner Ski Ranch Lodge, where you take off your skis to walk up the

*Clair Tappaan Lodge is the Sierra Club's retreat near Donner Pass*

road (east) to Donner Spitz Hutte. Turn right at this lodge onto an unplowed, narrow road, get your skis on, and head into backcountry to the summit of Mount Lincoln, which is above the Sugar Bowl Ski Area. Great for strong skiers, this trip doesn't require as much skill as fitness and should not be skied solo. In spring fit skiers can continue south along Squaw Ridge to the Sierra Club's Benson Hut. With firm corn snow, nature's own grooming makes the Benson Hut trip skiable on skating skis—only for really competent skaters. If you're a strong but less-expert skier, use metal-edged backcountry skis. The return trip takes you down Sugar Bowl's longest, easiest run. After the area has long been closed, it's blissful.

## Warning

_People skiing the backcountry routes I've just described should be properly equipped for emergencies, carrying food and water, the relevant US Geological Survey map (available from CTL), a flashlight, and a compass. They should also let management at any place they're staying know the intended route._

## Keep in mind

Cross-country skiers may not park in the Donner Ski Ranch parking lot without purchasing their lift ticket for that day. Norm Sailer, President of the Ski Ranch Corporation and friend to all skiers, has always been generous to "skinny skiers" passing through his area. He'll let you ski through without charge if you're not using the lifts. Years ago, Norm coined the phrase "Norpine" for free-heel skiers who used ski lifts—telemarking on heavier gear than most cross-country skiers use. He was also the first person in the whole Tahoe Region to allow snow boarding at his resort. In relation to the skiing facilities offered, Donner Ski Ranch's lift prices are the best in California.

## *The Concept of Shared Skiing Resources*

In 1978 I drove out to California from New England in MOR-BID, an elegant, '72 black Cadillac hearse with an unusual license plate. I had on board 12 pairs of wooden Bonna skis with three-pin bindings, bamboo poles, and 20 pairs of light-weight leather shoes—all in good condition. "Morbid" had come with the hearse and did not describe my mood; I had the gear and the opportunity to start my own Nordic ski school at Soda Springs-Norden. I'd been told by a friend, a Sierra Club member in the Bay Area, that the club's rambling mountain lodge in the Sierra needed one.

On the Friday evening of my first weekend at Clair Tappaan Lodge, I showed my super-eight documentary of the

*In the winter of '81 when 841" of snow fell, the author skied off the lodge roof*

*Five Easy Turns* that make cross-country skiing so enjoyable. The next morning at 5 A.M., one enthusiastic volunteer and I stamped out on snowshoes a teaching piste on a moderate downhill slope. After breakfast, 35 people who had watched my film (most had their own equipment) signed up for a lesson, and only two of these asked for a refund on seeing the crowd. Since I had no skiing assistant, a morning and an afternoon class were in order. But no one would have it that way; they all wanted a lesson there and then! So we worked together. As better skiers surfaced they became my demonstrators whose movements I critiqued. That lesson went on for well over two hours, before I ran out of steam. On Sunday morning there were three more volunteers to stamp out trails and another huge class.

    The season after establishing the school, I opened another door. Without giving notice to the lodge committee, the newly appointed lodge manager took off with his girlfriend. I was invited to assume his responsibilities, and the next eight years of my life were lived at Clair Tappaan Lodge. When my assistants (by now I had a teaching staff) and I wanted to groom snow with a machine to make a better ski-school area and 12 kms of trails, we encountered some resistance. But snow is so deep and moist here most of the winter that there could be no gliding over it; you just clumped around and called it skiing. Even snowshoeing to pack the trails before skiing could make all the difference. Eventually, there was enough enthusiasm to start grooming with a good, used machine that I persuaded the Sierra Club to purchase from Royal Gorge Resort.

My best instructor, Bill Aaron, took over the ski school when I left for the Bay Area, and after a few years Herb Holden took over from Bill. Herb has run the school for the past eight years and was recently appointed lodge manager. A grand new scheme will link the CTL skiing trails to Auburn Ski Club's trails on the other side of Boreal Ridge (when the snow base is good enough). A route from Auburn Ski Club via Clair Tappaan Lodge to Donner Ski Ranch, where an afternoon lift ticket costs only $5 for a senior, is in the offing. After skiing to Donner Ski Ranch, you could spend the afternoon skiing there, and finish your day by skiing down to Clair Tappaan Lodge. (CTL informs me that this cooperative endeavor will begin with the first season of the new millennium.) ❅

# Area 6—At a Glance

## Alpine Skills International—Donner Spitz Hutte
ASI, Box 8, Norden, CA 95724
phone (530) 426-9108    fax (530) 426-3063

### Distance From
Los Angeles—404 mi.    Fresno—304 mi.       San Jose—254 mi.
Bay Area—189 mi.       Sacramento—89 mi.    Reno—58 mi.

### Elevation & Facilities
Donner Pass—7,200'    No groomed trails    No dogs

A backcountry ski school, with groomed slopes next to ASI at Donner Ski
Ranch for Telemark and Nordic/Alpine instruction.

### Destination Lodging
72 beds available, mostly dormitory bunk rooms; 5 private rooms, double
occupancy.

### Alternate Lodging
For snow emergencies in Colfax, Auburn, & Nevada City (see "Where to stay
and eat" [Chap. 6], page 40).

### Prices
Dormitory bunk & breakfast $25. Private room (double occupancy) & break-
fast $80. Dinner $12. Breakfast for non-guests $7. Day-use of lodge $5, with
night parking $10.

### Ski School
ASI offers a broad series of technical clinics for all mountaineering skills, year-
round. Winter program includes snowboarding, rescue, and avalanche clinics
taught by Norm Wilson. For program and backcountry-ski-rental prices contact ASI.

# AREA 6. ALPINE SKILLS INTERNATIONAL —DONNER SPITZ HUTTE

## Summary

Alpine Skills Institute (ASI) specializes in all ski-mountaineering skills rather than machine-groomed trails. Their inexpensive lodge is close to three down-hill ski areas as well as Royal Gorge. In ASI's comprehensive Nordic-teaching component they include track-skiing skills; elite racers such as US Champion Nancy Fiddler lead skating clinics here. Dormitory rooms are spacious, well designed, and clean, while private rooms are small and located in the quietest part of the lodge. This is an ideal place for either the serious telemark skier or a group of friends on a tight budget. The guiding service is led by the owners, Mimi and Bela Vadasz.

## How to get there

*From Sacramento* exit I-80 at Soda Springs-Norden and drive 4 miles east on Donner Pass Rd. to Donner Spitz Hutte on your right. *From Reno* exit I-80 at Donner Pass Rd., which parallels Donner Lake and I-80 after Truckee. (Except during blizzards, there's no need to continue west on I-80 as far as the Soda Springs-Norden exit.) Continue 7 miles west on Donner Pass Rd. as it climbs the pass. Donner Spitz Hutte is on your left as you come over the pass.

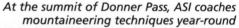

*At the summit of Donner Pass, ASI coaches mountaineering techniques year-round*

## Description of area

The alpine area including Donner Peak, Mt. Judah, and Mt. Lincoln to the south and Boreal Ridge and Castle Peak to the north is the ASI playing field. Across the road from their lodge, Donner Ski Ranch is the controlled training ground Mimi and Bela use for coaching their clients. Here they teach both tele-mark and parallel-skiing techniques on backcountry skis, preparing students for the rougher, natural conditions they'll ski in the wilderness.

Like Clair Tappaan Lodge down the road, ASI is ideally situated for immediate access to hundreds of square miles of wilderness skiing. In the spring this territory undergoes a snow phase where nature does all the grooming, and wilderness skating has become a new way to enjoy these conditions. On the Sierra Crest 1,100 feet above Donner Lake, with the Pacific Crest Trail traversing the parking lot, Donner Spitz Hutte has no rival as an alpine base. (The USGS 7.5-minute Norden quadrangle is available at the front desk.)

## Warning

*People skiing backcountry routes should be properly equipped for emergencies, carrying food and water, the relevant US Geological Survey map, a flashlight, and a compass. They should also let management at any place they're staying know the intended route.*

## To Anderson Peak under Spring Conditions

For an adventurous skiing weekend in spring (and in some good snow years well into summer), Donner Spitz Hutte is ideal. Leave the lodge and head south to Mt. Lincoln by traversing fairly high across the western slopes of Donner Peak and Mt. Judah. You can't ski the top of the ridge late in the season because the snow will have evaporated up there. A few tree-shaded stretches on your route, where the sun doesn't get to the snow, will be icy and may intimidate you. If so, gain ground by skiing above, not below them. But if you can, take the more interesting, direct route.

By setting your metal-edged skis, equally weighted and parallel, on their uphill edges with the lower ski slightly ahead, you get a grip on the ice and maintain balance. Now, vailing your stomach, glide downhill just enough for gravity to help you, and quickly traverse the icy section. Don't even think of bailing out here; the mere thought can take the cutting edge off your skis.

You'll be skiing on Sugar Bowl territory as you approach the summit of Mt. Lincoln, and you can save time by traversing its eastern shoulder. This shortcut places you at roughly 8,000 feet on Squaw Ridge heading toward Tinker Knob, where prairie falcons breed each summer. Although you can't see it until you're very close, the Sierra Club's Benson Hut is only 5 kms ahead. Behind this hut is Anderson Peak, your goal now as it has been mine many times. You can write your name and the date of your ascent and put it in the steel box at the top. Walt Disney did, but someone has since stolen his autograph.

*The author on lightweight touring skis, carrying two light packs for a well-balanced load on a solo trip*

Anderson Peak is special because of the uniform, 40° pitch of its north face—perfect for steep telemarking. Climbing on skis, you circle it from the west until you're almost at the summit. You have to take your skis off to reach the top at 8,683 feet. If your timing is right, there'll be a steep, narrow tongue of snow just below the summit on the north face, over which you can start your downhill rush to Benson Hut, directly below you. "Gnarly," describes the induction to this descent. You might want to sideslip for the first few feet. Once you are off the tongue, the open face of Anderson is steep but broad, and there are no rock outcrops to grab you.

In late July 1983, I brought my Kids Course to Anderson Peak along this route. We had a 10-month ski season that year after more than 800 inches of snow fell between October and April. These boys and girls were all about 14 years old, and only two of them could make turns on Anderson. While they were too light to control the corn snow on such steep ground, what a trip we had! With mountain bluebirds as avian company, we slept at Benson Hut and telemarked every slope we came to along the west side of Squaw Ridge. ❄

# Area 7—At a Glance

### Auburn Ski Club— Training Center
Auburn Ski Club, Box 829, Soda Springs, CA 95728
(530) 426-3313

### Distance From
| | | |
|---|---|---|
| Los Angeles—402 mi. | Fresno—302 mi. | San Jose—252 mi. |
| Bay Area—187 mi. | Sacramento—87 mi. | Reno—56 mi. |

### Elevation & Facilities
| | |
|---|---|
| Trails and Day Lodge—7,100' | Groomed—15 kms |
| 50-meter Nordic ski jump | Biathlon rifle range |
| Boreal Ski Area lifts | |

### Training Center
There are two professionally coached training programs—Nordic and Alpine.
**Nordic includes:** Jr. Nordic Development Team; Jr. Cross-country Race Clinics; Club Instruction Days; Citizen Racing Program; Biathlon Competition; & Ski Jumping.

### Membership
Primarily a Training Center—well organized for teaching and holding competitive Nordic events—that anyone may join.

### Prices
Basic club membership is $20 per year. Members only may purchase a $60 full-season trail pass ($30 for new members, junior 18-/senior 65+ free season pass). Youth and race team Dec-April $60. Jr. Development Team coached Oct-April for $300. Jr. Race Clinics, 6 sessions for $20.

### Lodging
Closest, Boreal Lodge at the foot of the ski area; on Donner Pass Rd., are Clair Tappaan Lodge & Donner Spitz Hutte. Truckee is 8 miles east on I-80.
**Special comment:** Auburn Ski Club is unique in its promotion and coaching—particularly—of young people in every discipline of skiing. It is a family-oriented operation that fills gaps not covered by commercially operated areas.

# 9   TAHOE REGION
# BOREAL RidGE

## AREA 7. AUBURN SKI CLUB—TRAINING CENTER

### Summary

Only the Olympic site at Lake Placid has a comparable training center to offer young skiers for learning and developing Nordic skiing skills at minimal expense. Auburn Ski Club's fine lodge has been directed by Bill Clark for 20 years. The club has Alpine as well as Nordic programs which, offered at non-commercial rates, are boons to parents with ski-minded offspring. Among the disciplines taught are: Track Racing on a respected (technically difficult) 15-km course; Slalom Coaching and Racing on Boreal's downhill slopes; and Biathlon, which combines rifle marksmanship with cross-country racing. Also taught is the rarefied winter sport of Ski Jumping, a specialty of the Finns; there are more Finns flying through the air, using giant skis for loft than other Nordic nationalities. At Auburn Ski Club, all these disciplines are taught to boys and girls from ages 6 to 18. Family involvement is very much part of the program; there's a lot of volunteering by parents to help run the events.

### How to get there

*From Sacramento or Reno* exit I-80 at Boreal, 8 miles west of Truckee and 50 miles east of Auburn. Drive west through the parking lot of Boreal Ski Area to the Auburn Ski Club Training Center parking lot.

69

## Description of area

Winding up and down pine-clad hills at the foot of Boreal Ridge are 15 kms of immaculately groomed trails. Auburn Ski Club's trails, which combine tracks for striding and a skating lane, are all set for cross-country training and racing. Not your casual, drop-in commercial touring resort, Auburn is a well-run training center, whose Nordic director is Sally Jones. All programs here are designed to be coeducational, which means the girls get into the high-flying ski-jump act, too.

If you look uphill, south of the large, modern Day Lodge, you'll see the club's own 50-meter ski-jumping hill. No, the hill isn't only 50 meters high. With a natural hill, or a giant ramp designed to simulate a hill for ski jumping, the declared measurement (50 meters in this case) is the anticipated safe distance for the skier to be in free flight. Wind force and direction are special dangers to ski jumpers; another is a run down the ramp so fast that it launches the jumper farther than can be safely flown. Of two impressive ski-jumping events in the Olympics, the larger is 90 meters with a proposed free flight the distance of a football field.

There is enough open ground close to the parking lot to set up a 50-meter rifle range on the snow, and biathletes fire their rifles here when they're training. At safely spaced intervals each skier races several kilometers before reaching the range to fire at five tiny disks, one shot per disk, from 50 meters

*The Auburn Ski Club at Boreal is the premier Nordic training center in California*

Daphne Hougard

away. If a disk doesn't go down, a biathlete has to ski a short penalty circuit—adding precious time—for each target missed. Biathlon skiing requires brain as well as brawn: biathletes must pace themselves to arrive calm enough to shoot well. During the race each competitor shoots twice, once standing, the other time prone. Having set out individually, the skier with the fastest time wins.

The Auburn Ski Club's area is small but intensively busy. On Boreal's adjacent downhill slopes Auburn's Alpine coaches teach slalom technique and slalom racing. Since Auburn owns the ridge on which Boreal Ski Area is operated, the club's programs use the facilities. Ownership also provides much-needed money to subsidize the club's multifaceted educational programs.

## The Not-For-Profit Contribution to Skiing

There is a dimension to cross-country skiing in California that's almost missing. Where can you load your skis and go somewhere safe to work out without incurring a steep cost? "Safe" means a place you won't get lost, are unlikely to get hurt, and will be able to glide on a groomed trail. Besides the Auburn Ski Club and Clair Tappaan Lodge (CTL), there's only one place in the whole Tahoe Region where you can do this without first going to the bank. If you are 70 years old you can ski for free at Tahoe Donner Cross Country, a non-profit community project just north of Truckee (see Area 8).

I'm not suggesting you shouldn't pay a trail fee at any of the cross-country areas in the Tahoe Region. But if you have only a couple morning hours in which to ski, you need a half-day pass valid in the morning. Because most half-day passes don't go into effect until afternoon, you're out of luck. Some don't become effective until 1:30 P.M., by which time the snow can be very soggy. Furthermore, is there a program anywhere that charges half price for a half-day pass? Marketing strategies that ignore client use-patterns and needs cannot be maximizing profit.

I also suggest that price schedules reading "Free skiing over 70," read "Free skiing over 65." Do the math; how many people over 65 are going to use your trails scot-free? If you treat your old-timers well they become your best public-relations advocates—for free. Most likely they've been paying full price for more years than anyone else has. And let kids under 12 years ski free, because you want them to grow into the sport; many will become lifetime cross-country skiers and boost your long-term client base. Royal Gorge is already doing

*A biathlon racer from the University of Nevada at Reno and one from the University of Alaska competing here*

this, and Tahoe Donner offers free skiing to kids under 10 years old.

It's important that non-commercial operations like the Auburn Ski Club and less-than-commercial operations like the Sierra Club's Clair Tappaan Lodge set a standard not locked into profit. By creating programs that promote greater participation—particularly for the young and old—they improve the quality of people's lives. These two programs separately having limited trail mileage will benefit considerably by linking their trails. This Nordic interconnect trail is going to happen and will automatically open up further possibilities.

The third player in this interconnecting trail is Norm Sailer, always innovative at Donner Ski Ranch. Not only does he recognize that 65 years is old enough to earn a break, Norm's $5 afternoon lift ticket encourages older people to ski. By connecting the dots, you can start skiing from Auburn Ski Club, take a break at CTL (the dining room is open all day for tea), and have lunch at Donner Ski Ranch (with its excellent cafeteria and picnic tables) before an afternoon of telemarking. The ski back to your car at Auburn Ski Club or your lodging at CTL is mostly downhill. What a great Nordic day that will be! ❄

# Area 8—At a Glance

### Tahoe Donner Cross Country
11509 Northwoods Blvd., Truckee, CA 96161-6000
(530) 587-9484          www.tahoedonner.com

### Distance From
Bay Area—195 mi.          Sacramento—95 mi.          Reno—45 mi.

### Nearest Airport
Reno—45 miles. Serving all National airlines.

### Light Aircraft
Truckee Tahoe Airport—8 miles (non-commercial).

### Elevation, Facilities, & Hours
Trails—6,600' at Lodge, 6,500' at Euer Valley, 7,929' at Hawk's Peak
Groomed—100 kms          Telemarking at adjacent downhill area
Warming huts—4          No dogs          Snowshoeing
Hours—8:30 A.M.-5 P.M.

### Night skiing
Weds. & Sat. 5 A.M.-8 P.M., on 2.5-km loop.

### Passes & Rental Prices

|  | Adult (18-59) | Jr./Sr. (13-17/60-69) | Child (11-12) |
|---|---|---|---|
| Trail pass | $17 | $14 | $9 |
| Skis, boots, poles | $12 | $12 | $6 |
| Snowshoes | $15 | - | - |
| Pulk sled | $20 | - | - |

### Ski School

| | Adult/Jr. (18-59)/(13-17) | Sr./Child (60-69)/(7-12) |
|---|---|---|

**Full package** (includes 90-min. group lesson, equipment rental, trail pass)
$38          $29

Group track or skating lesson, 90 minutes $16.
Private lesson, 1 hour $30; each additional person $15.
**Tiny Tracks Snow School:** ages 5-9 years, weekends, and holidays only, 2-hour morning or afternoon; one session $25, both sessions $40.

### Lodging & Food
Contact Truckee-Donner Chamber of Commerce at (530) 587-2757, or North Lake Tahoe Resort Assoc. at (800) 824-6438. Truckee Hotel and Best Western (on Hwy. 267) are the closest accommodations. Truckee has many restaurants, including Sizzler for kids. The Day Lodge at the ski area has a dining room, sundeck, and cafeteria.

# 10   Tahoe Region

# Truckee

## AREA 8. TAHOE DONNER CROSS COUNTRY

### Summary

This cross-country ski area is operated by the Tahoe Donner Association. Tucked out of sight just north of Truckee, it occupies 4,800 acres of beautiful terrain with 100 kms of groomed tracks covering three track systems and 39 trails. The grooming for striding and skating is outstanding, with emphasis on easy, short one-way loops for parents skiing with small children. (You don't have to avoid skiers coming the other way.) Two excellent skiers manage Tahoe Donner, which is definitely one of the best learning centers in California. It is the only area with a night-skiing program under sodium-vapor lights. In the summer Tahoe Donner Cross Country becomes an equitation center.

### How to get there

*From Sacramento or Reno* take I-80 to Truckee, exiting at Donner Pass Rd. Turn left (east) and continue to the traffic light opposite the high school. Turn left (north) onto Northwoods Blvd. and go 4 miles. Turn right on Fjord Rd. and left on Alder Creek Rd. In a short distance the Equitation & Cross-country Skiing Center is on your left. You have to drive into the parking lot before you can see the Day Lodge. *From Tahoe City* take Hwy. 89 north to Donner Pass Rd. in Truckee. Turn left (west) and continue to the traffic light opposite the high school. Turn right (north) onto Northwoods Blvd. and continue as above.

*This French-Canadian Bombardier is one of the machines used to groom the Tahoe Donner Cross Country trails*

## Description of area

A Nordic skiing area created by Glenn Jobe, a former Olympic biathlete and the founder of Kirkwood Cross Country Ski Center, is likely to be good. The original layout of trails, the quality of trail grooming, and the ski school today under Andrew Hall's direction continue to draw people. Trails are wide, with plenty of variety in the terrain. The easiest trails, marked with green blazes, are close to the lodge and are skied in one direction only, an aid to beginners and parents with small children. The ski school area in front of the lodge is one of the best designed for its purpose. With such breadth and length it's not overcrowded at lesson time. You have room to extend the technique you are learning without constantly having to stop and turn around.

In an area of almost 5,000 acres there are three trail systems: **Home Range**, **Sunrise Bowl**, and **Euer Valley**. You've got many options for both distance and terrain to chose from, using your area map or the huge panoptic map of the area mounted outside the lodge. If you prefer easy trails and don't want to ski far, you stay on the Home Range. If you want easy trails but would like to go a distance, head out to Euer Valley. It's very picturesque, and you can make Coyote Hut your goal. For a high-ground route, summitting at Hawk's Peak (7,929'), follow the blue blazes into the Sunrise Bowl System. Blue falls between green and black on the trail severity scale. If you venture to Drifter Hut on the high ground you'll encounter some black-trail skiing.

A very good, 25-km **California Day Trip** combines numerous trails from all three systems. You can get maps and advice for this route at the Day Lodge. Since 25 kms is about 15 miles, you'll need to carry food as well as drinks on this one. Tahoe Donner's other specialty is that it's the only cross-country ski area in California offering a well-lighted trail for night skiing. It operates from 5 to 8 P.M. on Wednesdays and Saturdays. Make sure to have a warm jacket with you because the temperature in this part of California can vary at least 30° between noon and nightfall.

## Where to stay and where to eat

The Tahoe Donner Association has many condos available during the ski season, (530) 587-9484. There are numerous hotels 8 miles away in Truckee.

The restaurants I prefer in Truckee are **The Passage** in the Truckee Hotel, and **Cottonwood** on Hwy. 267, just as you leave "Old Truckee," heading southeast. There are several other good restaurants and plenty of diners in Truckee. Parents with children who ski regularly in this area and have lots of kids were delighted when **Sizzler** came to the shopping center at the junction of Donner Pass Rd. and Hwy. 89.

## *Serendipity on Skis*

Unsure of my skiing ability at the start of the 98-99 season, I headed to the Tahoe Donner Cross Country Ski Center. I like the trail layout and knew the elevation wouldn't be too much of an adjustment. (I live at sea level these days.) Since the drive up from the Bay Area had been very warm, I was wearing sturdy sandals without socks as I walked from my truck over the snow to get a trail pass. The air was nice and cool for my feet. As I passed two fit-looking elderly people getting ready to ski, I saw that all their equipment was high-performance stuff—the latest Salomon skating boots, the finest skating skis, and carbon-fiber poles—the same gear that was in my own truck. And their ski outfits were knockouts, like the colorful Lycra bodysuits I wore as a racer. Anyway, they both looked a lot sharper than I was going to, that day.

Walking by them in sandals, lightweight wind pants, and T-shirt, I said cheerfully and purely for fun, "Gosh! I wish I had some fancy boots like yours." The woman, putting on her bright, bright yellow Salomon's, looked up, saw my bare toes against the white snow, and said severely, "You can, if you go out and buy them." She may have thought I was about to ask for some spare change.

I laughed and said, "I'm joking, I do have gear just like yours but I prefer sandals for driving. Do you have any idea

*Andrew Hall, director of cross-country skiing on the well-groomed tracks at Tahoe Donner*

how much a trail pass costs these days? I haven't bought one for years." Now both smiled warmly and the man said, "We don't need to know that. We're over 70 and we get a free pass. That's why we come here." However fit they were, now I knew they were older than me. It was great to hear about the free pass because older people should be encouraged to get out and ski. As I continued toward the Day Lodge, I thought how *langlaufers do* live longer.

Later that afternoon, I watched these same two skiers out on the ski school area where they were practicing skating; they were quite good at it. Having skied a few kilometers by this time, I started practicing variations of modern skating techniques. The two skiers stopped to watch me, and after a while I went over to chat with them. It was a lovely sunny afternoon. They told me they were 72 and 73 years old, and we talked on about the finesse of skating. Soon we were having a little clinic together. Again I was impressed with the unhurried smoothness of their skiing. Later I asked if I might take their photo for this book I'm writing, which led to a serendipitous discovery.

"Who's your publisher?" the woman asked. And when I told her "Wilderness Press," she was delighted. "That's my brother Tom, he's your publisher," she said. I knew then that her brother is Tom Winnett. He's the publisher who started Wilderness Press, and now his daughter Caroline is my publisher. As we parted I said, "Give Caroline a call when you get home; tell her you met one of her authors hard at work." We had a good laugh.

I couldn't help thinking how life is like skiing along a series of interconnecting trails. Each trail is an out-and-back route to be explored randomly or a loop route that connects to other circles. I've lived numerous lives that have become linked, like the five circles of the Olympic flag at Squaw Valley. This flag and its accompanying flame will greet me as I turn off Hwy. 89 for my next set of trails. ❄

# Area 9—At a Glance

### Resort at Squaw Creek/Olympic Valley
Box 3333, Olympic Valley, CA 96146
(530) 583-6300    www.squawcreek.com

### Distance From
Bay Area—200 mi.    Reno Tahoe International Airport—42 mi.
Lake Tahoe—6 miles.

### Elevation, Facilities, & Hours
Trails—6,000-6,200'    Groomed—18 kms    Snowshoeing
No dogs    Horse sleighing    Hours—8:30 A.M.-5 P.M.

### Passes & Rental Prices

|  | Adult (14-61) | Sr. (62-72) | Child (6-13) |
|---|---|---|---|
| Trail pass | $13 | $6 | $8 |
| **Rentals** |  |  |  |
| striding | $15 | $9 | $6 |
| skating | $20 | $20 | $20 |
| **Snowshoes** | $12 | $12 | $12 |
| **Snowshoeing** (trail pass only) |  |  |  |
|  | $6 | - | - |

### Ski School
Group lesson, 1 hour $30. Same lesson, with rentals, $35.
Private lesson, 1 hour $35; each additional person $25.
Skating clinic by appointment only $40, with rental $45.

### Lodging & Food
This is a destination resort offering deluxe rooms, suites, and penthouses. For rooms and suites the price range is from $325 to $525. Penthouses are from $550 to $1,900. The resort hotel has five indoor dining choices and a sundeck barbecue area; there's live music during the day.

### Swimming & Ice skating
A large, heated outdoor swimming pool (open day and night) and skating rink are on site.

### Shopping Mall
The resort has its own shopping mall selling ski clothing and accessories.

# SQUAW VALLEY

## AREA 9. RESORT AT SQUAW CREEK/OLYMPIC VALLEY

### Summary

The Resort at Squaw Creek is a luxury conference resort and a completely self-contained leisure destination. On its 400 acres is a golf course that becomes a cross-country skiing area in winter. The resort development cost, completed at some $130 million in 1990, gives an idea of the luxury you may anticipate. Both the cross-country skiing program with 18 kms of groomed trails and the downhill lift directly accessing Squaw Valley's Alpine skiing are available as you walk out the door. If you're staying at the resort, this convenience is extremely attractive. With a wonderful view the full length of Olympic Valley to Squaw Peak, the heated outdoor swimming pool and ice rink are something else. But be aware that lift tickets and trail passes are not included in your accommodation fee, and the cross-country program lies low on the resort's list of priorities.

### How to get there

*From either the Bay Area or Reno*, exit I-80 onto Hwy. 89 at the Squaw Valley exit in Truckee. Drive 8 miles south toward Tahoe City and, following the sign for Squaw Valley, turn right. The Olympic torch will be burning at this exit. After 0.5 mile bear left at the **Y**-junction toward the Resort at Squaw Creek. (If you're not staying at the resort, drive down the ramp and park in the main lot. Walk along the meadowside road to the resort's lower shopping mall and ski

81

*The Resort at Squaw Creek has every comfort and a commanding view of Olympic Valley*

shop.) If you're staying at the resort, drive to the hotel to unload. Then you can either make use of the valet parking or drive your car back to the lot.

## Description of area

Like Paradise and Heaven, Squaw Valley occupies the same location as Olympic Valley. Squaw Valley was famous long before the Olympic Games were held there. But since the games, Olympic Valley has become the parochial name for this Alpine-skiing location. The valley is a cul-de-sac hemmed in by steeply forested slopes and rougher, rock-strewn terrain above tree-line. The summit of 8,885-foot Squaw Peak and the gigantic gondola, carrying skiers to it, dominate the west end of the valley. No other ski area I have seen in the US or in Europe has topography that so clearly defines the two French phrases for skiing—*ski alpin* (skiing the mountain) and *ski de fond* (skiing the valley)—downhill and cross-country skiing, as we know them.

While the valley golf course used for the cross-country skiing program couldn't be more dramatically beautiful, its 6,000-foot elevation doesn't get a great snow base, and the Nordic season is much shorter than at most areas. Still, since no terrain with a shallow snow base is easier to groom than a golf course, I wonder why the grooming of this area was so shoddy on the three occasions I visited. (My visits were weeks apart, and the snow conditions for grooming on each occasion couldn't have been better.) While Squaw Valley's hotel resorts and downhill skiing can garner excellent ratings, its cross-country skiing area doesn't do justice to the remarkable setting.

## Chapter 11

## Lodging and food

A resort hotel of this size has all the facilities of a town, including an ice-skating rink, a heated outdoor swimming pool, four restaurants, a pub, a deli, and a wide variety of gift shops. The rooms and suites are luxurious (I've stayed in both on different occasions) and the food is good in the two restaurants where I've eaten, the Italian-style **Ristorante Montagna** and the American-style **Cascades**. Prices are commensurate with the high level of luxury being offered. In the ski season, overnight accommodations range from $325 for a small single room with a view to the rooftop Presidential Penthouse at $1900.

## *Ungraded Grooming*

On the three occasions that I skied the Resort at Squaw Creek, skating was made difficult because whoever had done the grooming didn't know how to best use the machine. One side of the track was consistently a foot lower than the other, and worse than this on corners and steep gradients. The diagonal striding tracks out were also poorly delineated.

There were numerous businessmen—always in pairs—holding animated discussions as they stomped the groomed trails, preferring the striding tracks because they are firmest. Every one of them was hacking his way round the trails in dainty walking shoes—most of the sort that don't have shoelaces. Having read the "Squaw Creek Skier's Responsibility Code," I knew that Rule 5 clearly states, "Do not enter a track unless you are on skis or snowshoes." Eventually I decided to broach this small detail with two delinquent characters approaching me. Intending to put them in the pencil sharpener, I said, "Please excuse me, but the skiing rules here state you may not..." and I spelled out my complaint.

"Ah!" said one of the two, a lawyerly looking fellow whose wingtips were cutting grooves as clean as deer slots in the packed snow. "We're not skiers are we, so we haven't read the Skier's Responsibility Code, have we?" ❄

# Area 10—At a Glance

## Tahoe Cross Country

Box 1926, Tahoe City, CA 96415
(530) 583-5475

## Distance From

| | | |
|---|---|---|
| Bay Area—215 mi. | Sacramento—115 mi. | Reno—40 mi. |
| Truckee—15 mi. | Kings Beach—5.5 mi. | Tahoe City—4 mi. |

## Elevation, Facilities, & Hours

| | | |
|---|---|---|
| Trails—6,300-7,700' | Groomed—65 kms | Warming hut—2 |
| No dogs | Snowshoeing | Pulk sleds |
| Hours—8 A.M.-5 P.M. | | |

## Passes & Rental Prices (free trail pass for children 6- and seniors 70+)

| | Adult (18-59) | Jr./Sr. (13-17/60-69) | Child (7-12) |
|---|---|---|---|
| Trail pass | $15 | $12 | $6 |
| Skis, boots, poles (all styles) | $15 | $10 | $9 |
| Demo skis (high tech) | $18 | $12 | - |

## Ski School

| | Adult | Jr. | Child | Sr. |
|---|---|---|---|---|
| Beginner's Special (includes equipment, group lesson, and full-day trail pass) | | | | |
| track | $38 | $30 | $25 | $30 |
| skate | $42 | $34 | $29 | $38 |

Group lessons 90-min. track $15; 1-hr. skating clinic $20.
Private lesson $25; additional person $15.

## Special Event

The Great Ski Race (March), the largest cross-country ski race in the West —30 kms from Lake Tahoe to Truckee via the Sawtooth Ridge.

## Lodging & Food

There are unlimited beds in the area at nearby motels, hotels, and lodges. Call the North Tahoe Resort Association at (800) 824-6348. There are also many restaurants—offering gourmet to plain fare—along Hwy. 28 (North Shore Blvd.) from Tahoe City to Kings Beach. The comfortable Day Lodge at Tahoe Cross Country has a pleasant dining room/lounge and serves Continental breakfasts, lunches, and snacks.

# 12  Lake Tahoe Region
# North Shore

## AREA 10. TAHOE CROSS COUNTRY

### Summary

Situated a half-mile above the north shore of Lake Tahoe (near Tahoe City High School), Tahoe Cross Country doesn't get as deep a snow base as some areas and may start the ski season a little later. Most of the groomed 65 kms are one-way trails with a variety of easy and more advanced routes. The ski school guides specialize in working with handicapped skiers, using routes of an intermediate standard. The Base Lodge with its wood stoves and a combined dining/sitting room has a collection of fine bird paintings and a particularly friendly ambiance.

Nothing is technically difficult at Tahoe Cross Country until the day of The Great Ski Race. The long route from Base Lodge to Truckee's Hilltop Lodge is Tahoe Cross Country's outstanding feature. This dramatic 30-km trail climbs over 1,000 feet out of the Tahoe Basin in the first 12 kms, and then heads slightly downhill along the Sawtooth Ridge all the way to Truckee. About 1,000 bold skiers participated in the race in 1999, including three whose arms did all the work the entire route (see "Strength, Courage, and Endurance" below).

### How to get there

*From Sacramento or Reno* leave I-80 at the Squaw Valley exit (Hwy. 89) in Truckee. Drive 11 miles south to Tahoe City. Bear left onto Hwy. 28 and drive 3 miles northeast to Dollar Hill. Turn left at the Shell station onto Fabian Way. Make the next right turn onto Village Dr. Go uphill and right-handed through an **S**-bend, and turn left onto County Club Dr. Tahoe Cross Country ski area is now on your left. Because of the high snow berm you may not see the lodge or parking lot; the second gap in the berm is the entrance to the ski area. *From South Lake Tahoe* follow Hwy. 89 north along the west shore of the lake to Tahoe City and continue as described above.

## Description of area

First developed by Skip Reedy, Tahoe Cross Country passed into the capable hands of Mike and Rose Wolterbeek, who redesigned the Day Lodge and maintained the close relationship with the local community. The very strong Truckee High School team trains and holds its races here; the elite Tahoe Nordic Search and Rescue Team puts on its annual fund-raiser—The Great Ski Race—here. For the 2000 season Kevin Murnane will be the new Tahoe Cross Country director.

The terrain is wooded pine forest, but not as densely packed with trees as most forests are around here. Trails are named for animals and birds of the local environment: Goshawk, Woodpecker, Quail, Redtail, and Eagleview. This trail was designed to give you a good workout rewarded by a view of Lake Tahoe. Chipmunk, Fox, Jackrabbit, and Bobcat are the easiest trails, closest to the lodge. With a more difficult rating and farther from the lodge there's a Bear Trail, too. I have a relevant tale: Once, many years ago I was skiing it in the early spring and found I had that bear for company. A big black fellow, he was snowshoeing on bearpaws dead ahead of me on the trail. I just slowed down and took the next exit.

By heading west on Porcupine Trail from its junction with Eagleview, you can pick up **The Great Ski Race** route that goes as far north as Truckee.

*From right to left, Candace Cable, Mark Wellman, and Bill Bowman in The Great Ski Race—Candace broke 2 hours for the 30 kms course, and won*

While this trail is packed for snowmobilers beyond Tahoe Cross Country's boundary, you're allowed to ski it. But to enjoy this route it's best to wait till March, when it's perfectly groomed in preparation for the annual epic.

You don't need to be a great skier to participate in The Great Ski Race, but you do need to be fit. Otherwise, you won't enjoy it and you become a liability. Most participating skiers are local people who wouldn't claim to be good skiers (though many are). They're healthy ski-enthusiasts, and some may take five to six hours to cover the 30-km (18-mile) distance. The men's record is Ben Husaby's 1 hour, 10 minutes—skating of course; and the women's record is Nancy Fiddler's 1 hour, 22 minutes. Astonishing times!

## Where to stay and eat

Between **River Ranch** on the Truckee River and **The Holiday House** at Tahoe Vista are many lodging choices. These two accommodations get my vote, but a call to the North Tahoe Resort Association's reservation service will open many other doors, (800) 824-6348. While local restaurants are too numerous to list, here are my preferences. Notwithstanding the high gourmet standard all around Lake Tahoe, one of the best culinary teams (offering "wild food from land and sea") is at **Truffula**, on North Lake Blvd. Larry and Kristi (chef and pastry chef), with their impeccable serving staff of two, will titillate your tastebuds and satisfy your appetite. Their cooking took me back 30 years to *Gaston et Gastonette* in Villefranche. One of the waiters, who is French, told me he knew this restaurant and that it's still good.

Next door to The Holiday House in Tahoe Vista are two excellent restaurants: **Cap'n Jon's** and **Le Petit Pier**. Both have excellent midweek specials. All along North Lake Blvd. are many pleasant restaurants, but the best skier's breakfast can be found at the **Crosswinds Cafe** in Kings Beach. You'll sit surrounded by owner Mike Benoist's museum-quality aviation photographs. And what Mike's wife, Chris, puts on the table is just as praiseworthy.

## *Strength, Courage, and Endurance*

Every March (for the past 23 years) a spirited fund-raiser in support of the Tahoe Nordic Search and Rescue Team takes place: The Great Ski Race. From the Tahoe Cross Country Base Lodge the route climbs 7 miles onto Sawtooth Ridge and then makes a long swoop down to the Hilltop Lodge in Truckee. It's a sprint for the elite skiers—a marathon for the majority. With over 900 people participating in 1999, this is the largest and certainly the most popular Nordic ski race in the West. Rescue team members and many community supporters organize the 30-km race. The proceeds help purchase equipment and otherwise support winter-survival and avalanche-education programs taught by the team's over 100 active members. Though I've skied the event several times and it's one of my favorite courses, this year—not fit enough to race and needing photos—I watched.

I planted the word "spirited" in the first sentence to suggest what the race is about. Racing always has to do with spirit: your personal performance is *you* under a microscope for as long as it takes to finish your race. You get to take stock and cannot hide from how you are performing. Other participants get to gauge you, too, but only you have the complete fact sheet. You may do better or less well than others perceive. Citizen races may have mass starts but they have single finishes.

How can you know, viscerally, what Strength, Courage, and Endurance it takes to ski the 30 kms to Truckee sitting over your skis and propelling yourself the entire distance using only your arms? Look at the three athletes doing this and consider working those mini ski poles. Imagine double-poling up that 1,000-foot climb over the first 7 miles of The Great Ski Race. It boggles the mind. In 1999, my three favorite warriors took the guise of three skiers you see pumping away at the start of the race. Look what power, energy, and

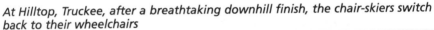

*At Hilltop, Truckee, after a breathtaking downhill finish, the chair-skiers switch back to their wheelchairs*

focus they are exerting in the first few meters. While all three will tumble and roll and pick themselves upright many times during the race, they will maintain competitive intensity for 30,000 meters—till they cross the finish line in Truckee.

Candace Cable, Mark Wellman, and Bill Bowman finished the race in the order you see them. Candace broke 2 hours for the course, and Mark and Bill were about 10 minutes back. While this was Mark's third finish in the race, in both previous runs he was the lone ranger. He is well known for his ascents of El Capitan and Half Dome. Candace is a six-time winner of the Boston Marathon in her wheelchair—her strength-to-weight ratio is phenomenal. Besides teaching downhill skiing skills, Bill is the US National Champion at handicap water-skiing. ❄

# Area 11—At a Glance

### North Tahoe Regional Park—Snow Play Area
Box 139, Tahoe Vista, CA 96140
(530) 546-4212

### Distance From
Tahoe City—19 mi.    Truckee—12.4 mi.
Kings Beach—2.4 mi.   Tahoe Vista—1 mi.

### Elevation, Facilities, & Hours
Trails—6,232-7,200'    Groomed—10 kms
                     (plus access to backcountry trails)
Sledding hills—2     Dogs welcome      Hours—8 A.M.-5 P.M.

### Prices
The Snow Play Area is free to local residents. There is a parking fee and trail fee. Children's sleds can be rented on-site. There are no skiing rentals on-site; nearest rentals are 2 miles away in Kings Beach at Tahoe Bike & Ski, 8499 North Lake Blvd., (530) 546-7437.

### Children & Dogs
The Snow Play Area is particularly set up for children's sledding and dogs exercising.

### Lodging & Food
There is no Day Lodge on-site, but there is a heated bathroom and a snacks concession. The Holiday House, (530) 546-2369, right on the lake in Tahoe Vista, is the closest dog-friendly hotel, and the Snow Play Area is the perfect place to exercise dogs. There are outstanding restaurants and many cafes nearby in Tahoe Vista and Kings Beach.

*With groomed sledding hills and trails, the park also welcomes dogs*

# AREA 11. NORTH TAHOE REGIONAL PARK —SNOW PLAY AREA

## Summary

This community-oriented Snow Play Area is an almost free operation maintained by North Tahoe Regional Parks under the supervision of Ranger Kim Ingstad. A multiuse recreational area, it's machine groomed for snowmobilers, cross-country skiers, and hill sledders. No better place exists in the Lake Tahoe Region to take young children who aren't ready for skiing. The Snow Play Area is a family affair where parents maintain responsibility for their children's welfare. It's also a dog's playground, where dogs can be off the leash under their owner's control. While the 10-km groomed loop is not tracked for striding, it is good for skating—especially just after grooming. Via the loop you gain access to many more ungroomed trails on higher ground. On-site amenities include bathrooms, a snack bar, and a well-plowed parking lot.

## How to get there

*From Truckee* go 10 miles southeast on Hwy. 267 to Kings Beach. Turn right (west) on Hwy. 28 (North Lake Blvd.) for Tahoe Vista. In 1 mile turn right (north) onto National Ave. In 0.4 mile turn left onto Donner Rd; follow it 1 mile to the parking lot.

## Description of area

This is a useful workout area for the skier or snowshoer who has an hour or two in which to exercise and doesn't want to head first to the bank. Winding in and out of the forest, the 10-km loop is groomed well enough for skating or striding, though there is no set track for striding. Once the sun has been shining for a while, the lack of set track doesn't much matter because your skis will make their own. With good timing the groomed loop can present a fine skiing surface; but first thing in the morning it will be rock-hard.

The real value of this little area, managed by two veteran rangers, Kim Ingstad and Dave Shaw, is in providing skiers, parents with children, and dog owners the opportunity to enjoy the outdoors without going to a commercial ski area. Users can play in the snow at their own pace. In maintaining this facility, the Parks & Recreation Dept. is fulfilling its winter program responsibility to the public well. Without instructors, trail-pass checkers, or protocols, common sense prevails. Particularly for children, two lovely open-sledding slopes are groomed, with long run outs eliminating any risk of hitting trees. The steeper slope provides excitement for the sledders.

## Lodging and food

If you're in the Lake Tahoe Region to ski any of the major cross-country or downhill areas, you have a large choice of cabins, condos, motels, and B and Bs. You can solve your lodging needs ahead of time by calling the North Tahoe Resort Association reservation service at (800) 824-6348. If you're skiing northstar™, Diamond Peak, or Tahoe Cross Country (and particularly if you have dogs with you), the well-situated **Holiday House** in Tahoe Vista may be your best bet. Besides being a champion windsurfer and skier, innkeeper Alvina Patterson is totally dog friendly. Right next door to Holiday House are two of the best restaurants on Lake Tahoe: **Le Petit Pier** and **Cap'n Jon's**.

## *Snow Parks:*
## *Non-exclusive Public Recreation*

There are a number of Snow Parks in California for multipurpose recreational use. If they are machine groomed it is to accommodate the snowmobilers who abound in some areas. Groomed trails for snowmobilers also provide groomed trails for ski-skaters at no, or minimal, charge. I like it! "Who feeds the raven also provides for the sparrow," to paraphrase my friend the perennial W.S. (not a skier).

When I was researching this book in the Mammoth Lakes area I found two Snow Parks right off Hwy. 395. I didn't ski at them myself but local cross-country racers do. Several

*Holiday House innkeeper Alvina Patterson is a veteran
windsurfing and skiing instructor*

skiers whom I met at the Tamarack Lodge Marathon told me
they ski these areas to get in some skating miles.

Whatever California Snow Park you discover (there's
one on Eagle Mountain off I-80), find out when the grooming
machine is going out and ski the track before the snowmobilers arrive. Though I have no interest in mechanized sports, I
never knock snowmobiling; a snowmobiler will zoom over to
help me one day—if I break my leg. Every ski area uses snowmobiles for rescue work. Besides, snowmobiles were very useful in the days before the modern grooming machines, when
we used them to pull our track setters. ✳

# Area 12—At a Glance

### northstar-at-tahoe™ cross country, telemark, & snowshoe center
Box 129, Truckee, CA 96160-0129
(530) 562-2475        24-hr. snow phone (530) 562-1330
www.skinorthstar.com

### Distance From
Bay Area—206 mi.        Sacramento—96 mi.        Reno—40 mi.
Truckee—6 mi.        Kings Beach—6 mi.

### Nearest Airport
Reno—42 miles (all National Airlines)

### Light Aircraft
Truckee-Tahoe—3 miles (non-commercial). With 24-hr. notice northstar will pick you up at this airport, (530) 587-4119.

### Elevation, Facilities, & Hours
Trails—6,660-8,610'        Groomed—65 kms
telemark—Lift-served        Warming huts & picnic areas
No dogs        Snowshoeing throughout area
Hours—8:30 A.M.- 4 P.M.

### Passes & Rental Prices

|  | Adult (13+) | Child (5-12) |
|---|---|---|
| Trail pass (includes full use of Big Springs Gondola and Echo Chair) | | |
|  | $19 | $11 |
| Skis, boots, & poles (track/skating/telemark) | | |
|  | $19 | $10 (track only) |
| Snowshoes | $19 | $19 |

### Ski School
Many options for track skiing, skating, and telemarking. The focus is on teaching adults to ski. Learn-to-ski lesson $25; same lesson with trail pass and equipment $49. Improvement lesson $25 (inclusive $49). Learn-to-telemark lesson $25 (inclusive $49). Telemark-improvement lesson (requires P.M. lift ticket and lesson fee) $25. 1-hr. private lessons (Child or Adult) $40; each additional person $20.

### Lodging & Food
northstar-at-tahoe™ has more than 500 lodging units, (800) 466-6784. There are five restaurants of various styles in the destination Northstar Village, and the Cross Country Center has its own snack bar.

# Between Truckee & Kings Beach

## AREA 12. northstar-at-tahoe™ cross country, telemark, & snowshoe center

### Summary

This area's marketing identity prescribes that its name always be presented in lowercase letters (perhaps because it is 6 miles shy of Lake Tahoe?). Be that as it may, northstar is a well-known, downhill-skiing destination resort that includes a good Nordic program. Among the cross-country areas in California it is the leading telemark center. At 6,900 feet the Day Lodge is reached via the Big Springs Express Gondola, coming up from the village with downhill skiers. That you can use this lift all day for telemark skiing without extra charge is a bonus. The Cross Country Day Lodge has two trail systems, one on higher ground and more extensive than the other. Besides the lift-served telemark teaching program here, on full moon nights they feature barbecue suppers with night skiing.

### How to get there

*From Sacramento or Reno* exit I-80 at Hwy. 267 in Truckee and drive 6 miles southeast toward Kings Beach. *From Lake Tahoe* follow Hwy. 267 for 6 miles

*northstar-at-tahoe™ specializes in teaching telemark skiing in their Nordic program*

northwest of Kings Beach. Almost equidistant between the two on 267, north-star-at-tahoe™ requires no other routing. For the Cross Country Skiing Center, park in one of the many lots close to Northstar Village and purchase your cross-country pass at one of the village booths. This pass allows you onto the Big Springs Express Gondola, which takes you up to the Lodge at Big Springs. Get off here and head right, passing in front of two large buildings that block your view of the Cross Country Center.

## Description of area

For a cross-country skier the northstar logistical approach to its groomed Nordic area is both unique and fun. For the $19 price of your trail pass you may use the gondola all day and, if you want to ski telemark, the Echo Triple Chair is available as well. The Lodge at Big Springs, where you get off the gondola, is at 6,900 feet. A long way to your right, behind the two huge buildings you'll find the low, brown silhouette of the Cross Country Day Lodge. A blue-and-white banner to its left reads, NORTHSTAR CROSS COUNTRY & TELEMARK SKIING CENTER. The Day Lodge is comfortable and has its own cafe.

The trail map provided at the lodge illustrates two trail systems, of which the less extensive one branches west, around 7,000 feet in elevation. For the longer one, higher trails head east onto Sawmill Flat; from there you can climb to 7,850 feet on the High Country Trail. All of this area's 65 kms are groomed for striding and skating. As is typical of all other cross-country areas, you ski here on forest trails. But this area is uniquely situated in an alpine skiing area with many wide, groomed, intermediate downhill runs.

To take full advantage of northstar, go telemark skiing. "Bend ze knee, and you vill see how much you get for your trail fee," says Franz, an old Austrian friend of mine who likes to ski here. This Nordic program, long managed by Tom Couse, has a good telemark teaching program. If you become competent enough, you can take the Comstock Express (you'll need to buy a pass for it) to the summit of 8,610-foot Mount Pluto. Then take **The Plunge** (it's not *that* steep) down to Powder Bowl. While Mount Pluto's descending routes start out with black-diamond (most difficult) grading, they soon link up with less challenging blue routes. The new manager is Jennifer Noerdlinger.

## Where to stay and eat

northstar-at-tahoe™ is its own alpine village. With a pillow count of 5,500, there are more than 500 available on-site condos, cabins, and hotel rooms. For lodging at **Northstar Village** call (800) 466-6784. Five restaurants here offer fare ranging from fast food to elegant dining at the **Timbercreek Restaurant**. For off-site lodging, consider the **Truckee Hotel** (6 miles northwest on Hwy. 267) with its excellent restaurant, **The Passage**, or **Best Western**, only 1 mile short of Truckee (near the **Cottonwood Restaurant**). On Lake Tahoe there's the **Holiday House** in Tahoe Vista (head 6 miles southeast on Hwy. 267 to Kings Beach and go right a short distance on Hwy. 28). Holiday House has two of the best eateries on the North Shore next door to it, **Le Petit Pier** and **Cap'n Jon's**.

## *The Sound of Music*

At 8,610 feet, northstar's Mount Pluto bears a tantalizing and richly allusive name. Whoever named it wasn't thinking of Hades, Lord of the Dead, I hope. Perhaps they were thinking of the nymph ravished by Zeus, who became the mother of Tantalus. For his indiscretion on Olympus, this poor lad was made to stand chin-deep in water, hungry and thirsty, under a tree laden with succulent fruit he could almost reach. Or perhaps it was named to celebrate the ninth and outermost planet from the sun, discovered in 1930?

Returning to northstar in May because I'd not covered enough of its terrain on my midwinter visit, I had a rewarding experience on Mount Pluto. I went telemarking on the high ground. The Nordic skiing program here emphasizes its telemark program because the terrain is ideal and not too difficult for any good, intermediate skier. While there wasn't snow from the gondola base to Big Springs Lodge at 6,900 feet this late in the year, an unbroken snowbelt stretched from there to Pluto's summit at 8,610 feet. A 1,700-foot fall line on a 2-mile downhill run is very tantalizing for a telemark skier.

Lucky me! Over snow that hadn't been groomed for a month but had set up firmly beneath a soft surface, with lots of humps and sun cups to give it character, I didn't have to climb. Since Erin Burnell, northstar's Public Communications Manager, had got permission for me to "do my thing," Steve Harkinger, who happened to have work at the summit, rushed me to the top of Pluto on a snowmobile. (Don't knock snowmobiles when they're useful.) At the summit Steve suggested there was something worth seeing on the south side if I skied over the crest.

First I looked north with an eagle's-eye view down to Martis Lake and Prosser Reservoir, then across to Castle Peak, and the panorama was stunning. But on the south side of Pluto was California's translucent jewel of a lake shimmering more than 2,000 feet below me. I could see Lake Tahoe stretching south, 20 miles across the Tahoe Basin from Kings Beach to Heavenly Valley Ski Area. And for me that day half its alpine rim was a snow necklace of mountains strung around the horizon, framing the lake below and underpinning the blue sky.

On this south side of Pluto I found a small stone column with a tablelike top bearing an inlaid steel plate. An engraved map depicts Lake Tahoe with the California/Nevada boundary, and around the map's edge are words in praise of Lance Sevison, a boy aged 13 who died in a skiing mishap on the steep south slope below me. This evocative elegy reminded me of Rupert Brook's haunting line, "If I should die think only this of me...".

After eating lunch at this vantage point, it was time to try out my new equipment. Working with Fischer rep Dan Hill and Paco's Bike & Ski shop in Truckee, I was to evaluate the latest E 99—Fischer's lightweight backcountry ski. The Salomon backcountry boots and bindings designed to go with these skis were furnished by an old colleague, Bill Stirling, who is now the Salomon rep. Because of a film I'd made 20 years ago about telemark skiing on the original, Fischer green E 99s, I was awarded a two-year contract to test every cross-country ski design they make. At that time Bill was the Fischer rep in the Tahoe Region and we've kept in touch. So when I met Dan and Bill displaying their equipment at Royal Gorge in '99, they set me up with their latest telemark gear for spring skiing. With one painfully shaky ankle, the first thing that struck me about the new Salomon Greenland boot was its therapeutic firmness combined with comfort. We've come a long way since I made

*Taking The Plunge at northstar*

my film, when I used three-pin bindings and light, leather Galibier boots I could both hike and ski in.

So here I am on May 21, about to ski a delectable 1,700-foot fall line from Mount Pluto down to the Lodge at Big Springs. I'm using the best lightweight gear any classical telemarker could ask for, including new, backcountry SNS bindings. "Classical" means the old-fashioned way of tele-marking, as it does with striding the tracks. And now, as I swoop and glide, changing the leading leg to turn and turn— always completing them on this wide, open slope—I hear the sound of music and recognize French horns. My existential joy of movement to this music replenishes the precision I need for my unchecked descent. I don't miscalculate a turn as I stroke the constantly varying shapes of the mountain with my skis and respond to every change of the snow's texture. Never relin-quishing my initiative—playing with gravity, momentum, and balance—I link a hundred lyrical turns so that anyone seeing my route would be able to follow the score I've laid down on the snow.

Tough telemark, the modern way, with its short, sharp, aggressive turns, requiring much heavier boots and skis, is not for me. Rather than assault the hill with the clamor of a Mick Jagger, I'd sooner blend with it by listening to Amadeus while I ski. The harmonious horn concertos in E flat major are my favorite music; I loved to hear them played in London's Festival Hall by that late master of the horn, Dennis Brain. ❄

# Area 13—At a Glance

## Diamond Peak Cross Country & Snowshoe Center

Hwy. 431, Incline Village, NV 89451
phone (775) 832-1177    fax (775) 832-1281
www.diamondpeak.com

## Distances From

Reno—27 mi.    Tahoe City—20 mi.    Incline Village—6 mi.

## Nearest Airport

Reno/Tahoe (Incline Village is the closest Lake Tahoe Resort).

## Elevation, Facilities, & Hours

Trails—8,200-8,600'    Groomed—40 kms    Warming hut
Snowshoeing    Dogs on trails after 12:30 P.M.
Hours—9 A.M.-5 P.M.

## Passes & Rental Prices (free trail pass for children 5- and seniors 70+)

|  | Adult (13-59) | Senior (60-69) | Child (6-12) |
|---|---|---|---|
| Trail pass | $14 | $10 | $8 |
| Skis, boots, poles | $15 | $11 | $7 |

Adventure Pass includes trail pass plus unlimited interchangeable equipment
for skiing and snowshoeing $35. Wednesdays half price.
Dogs (after 12:30 P.M.) with pooper-scooper and on leash $3. Full-season dog
pass $25.

## Ski School

Beginner total package (ages 7 and up) $34. Group lesson $15.
Private lesson $25; each additional person $20.

## Lodging & Food

Numerous large hotels (Hyatt Regency etc.) between Stateline and Incline
Village. Many motels in Kings Beach, and Holiday House in Tahoe Vista. Call
(800) 468-2463 for all lodging reservations. Good restaurants abound in
hotel areas. Base Lodge has food and beverages.
**Special note:** This cross-country ski center is at a higher base level than other
areas in the region, so dress warmly.
**Parking:** Roadside parking in plowed lots on Hwy. 431, 5 miles north of junction with Hwy. 28.

# 14 Lake Tahoe Region
# North Shore-Nevada

## AREA 13. DIAMOND PEAK CROSS COUNTRY & SNOWSHOE CENTER

### Summary

Off Mt. Rose Highway (Nevada Hwy. 431), Diamond Peak, at 27 miles, is the closest cross-country skiing area to Reno's City Center. With trails all above 8,000 feet, it is particularly popular with local skiers from Lake Tahoe's North Shore (only 6 miles from Incline Village). Four designated snowshoe trails form a chain the full length of Diamond Peak's territory. After 12:30 P.M. leashed dogs are welcome, and they carry their own passes. The well-groomed trails involve more hill climbing than some areas. In the near future Diamond Peak Lodge will be relocated slightly, but the 1-mile-distant planned move won't affect the trails very much. Check with the program before going, especially if you don't know the area.

### How to get there

*From Reno* take Hwy. 395 south for 7 miles and then turn west on Hwy. 431 for MOUNT ROSE SKI AREA AND LAKE TAHOE. In 20 miles you'll see a sign for Diamond Peak Cross Country on the left side of the road. Park at roadside and look for the packed trail leading to the Day Lodge. *From Lake Tahoe* follow North Shore Blvd. (Hwy. 28) 1 mile west of Incline Village to the junction of Hwy. 431. Turn north and drive 5 miles up to the parking lot on your right. A shuttle-bus service

101

Diamond Peak

*Dogs are welcome afternoons and carry their own passes*

runs daily from Incline Village to the Diamond Peak Cross Country Center. For the schedule call (775) 832-1177.

## Description of area

At Diamond Peak you're on high ground in a fairly dense pine forest with wide, well-groomed trails. Clark's nutcrackers, jay-like mountain birds, will let you know vociferously that you're in their territory. Some of the Diamond Peak trails are designated easy, about half are intermediate, and the rest are advanced. If you're not an experienced skier, ski in the afternoon here because on cool mornings the grooming stays firm, which makes it harder to get a climbing grip. If you're a good skater, firm conditions are an asset; many local skiers make a point of training here.

For a beginner, a striding lesson close to the lodge will set you up to ski the uphill trail (it's not steep) called Easy Street. After 2 kms turn right onto the short B-Line Trail connecting you with Hawk's View. Go left on Hawk's View (a one-way route to be skied clockwise) to reach Diamond Peak. There's a picnic table here and a great view of Lake Tahoe. (An easy-to-follow map, which you can get at the lodge, illustrates another fine route for snowshoers to Diamond Peak.)

There's great off-trail telemarking in the spring corn snow at Diamond Peak, where meandering downhill through open glades is so inviting. You'll need heavier skis than your track or skating ones for this, and they can be rented at the Day Lodge. Fischer E 99s are ideal. Don't try this steeper off-trail terrain until you're competent at this sort of skiing, and don't do it alone. Since the trails are so wide here, you can always practice telemark turns without going off-trail. While it's fun going downhill off-trail, remember it's hard work climbing back up. So if you want to telemark off the trails, for your own safety discuss it with the staff at the Day Lodge first, where the ski-school director may even send you out with a guide.

**The management at Diamond Peak offers this guarantee: if you are not satisfied with the skiing conditions in the first hour of skiing, you will receive a voucher to come back another day—for free.**

## Where to stay and eat

Major hotels, motels, casinos, and B and Bs in the Incline Village, Stateline, and Kings Beach area are only a few miles away—as are many fine restaurants. If you're near Kings Beach, try the **Crosswinds Cafe** for a bumper breakfast. For retirees on an economy budget, check out the winter midweek special—Sunday through Thursday—at **Circus Circus** in Reno, with double-occupancy rates for as little as $34 per night; call (800) 648-5010 for reservations. It's a lovely drive over Mt. Rose Pass and Reno's only 27 miles away. The best Italian food in Reno is just across the street from Circus Circus—upstairs in **Harrah's**. You could ski by day and then return to "Goose City" to play.

## *Dogs Welcome*

Dogs pose a question for cross-country ski-area operators. People living in the mountains have dogs—usually large healthy dogs that need lots of exercise. Many dog owners are cross-country skiers and they want to exercise together with their dogs. But since most skiers don't want dogs around them on the tracks, area directors have a conundrum. A "No Dogs Allowed" policy solves the problem and is not unreasonable because the expense of grooming is for the benefit of skiers, not dogs. And after all, dogs are incontinent outdoors.

Some areas—usually smaller ones catering to a predominantly local clientele—have decided to accommodate skiers with their dogs. These dog-friendly areas typically designate a trail (or trails) for dog owners—sometimes shared with snowshoers. Shasta Ski Park Nordic Center has chosen this policy because snowshoers are less affected by rambunctious dogs than skiers who are quite easily put off balance. Without exception, those areas that allow dogs expect owners to have them under control by leash or harness and to carry plastic bags for you know what.

Director Kris Kosar at Diamond Peak has come up with a pro-dog solution, and a pleasing one. Since dogs are not allowed on the groomed trails until 12:30 P.M., the hard-core skiers, who usually prefer to ski in the morning, can get in their training before the dogs arrive. With dog handlers getting to ski all the trails after 12:30 P.M., Diamond Peak has made full recreational use of the area. Dogs can have their own season pass for $25 and carry their photo-identification on their collars, a savings benefit that also ensures best behavior. Pooper-scoopers are available at various points along the trails, and owners have the onus of using them. In three visits to this area, I saw not one pile of poop and lots of happy dogs.
❄

# Area 14—At a Glance

## Spooner Lake Cross Country Ski Area
Box 11, Glenbrook, NV 89413
phone (775) 887-8844   fax (775) 883-5684
spoonerlk@aol.com

### Distances From
Reno Airport—45 mi.    Tahoe City—25 mi.
Kings Beach—16 mi.    S. Shore State Line—12 mi.
Incline Village—11 mi.    Carson City—10 mi.

### Bus Service
From N. or S. Shore (3 per day) $5 round trip, call (530) 542-5900

### Elevation, Facilities, & Hours
Trails—7,000-7,823'       Highest off-trail elevation—9,214'
Groomed—65 kms       Overnight cabins on trails
No dogs                  ·Snowshoeing          Pulk sleds
Hours—9 A.M.-5 P.M. midweek (no entry after 4 P.M.)

**Passes & Rental Prices** (free trail pass for children 6- and seniors 70+)
Best packages and specials of any area; too many to list, get a brochure.

|  | Adult | Student (16-22) | Jr. (7-15) | Sr. (60-69) |
|---|---|---|---|---|
| Trail pass | $15 | $9 | $4 | $5 |
| Rental prices slide according to age group | | | | |
| track skis, boots, & poles | $15-$4 | | | |
| skating skis, boots, & poles | $21-$12 | | | |
| snowshoes | $15-$9 | | | |
| pulk sled | $15-$6 | | | |

## Ski School
Prices slide according to age group

Lesson (packages include equipment and trail pass)
**track**     $34-$18
**skating**   $39-$22
1-hour Private lessons $30; each additional person $15.

## Lodging & Food
Reno, Carson City, South Lake Tahoe, and Incline Village all have accommodations ranging from luxury hotels to good B and Bs. The closest restaurants and hotels are in Carson City (800) 638-2321, and Incline Village (800) 468-2463. These numbers provide full details about food and lodging in these two areas.
**Overnight cabins:** Spooner Lake has classic, hand-hewn Scandinavian-style log cabins—ski in, ski out, 1-3 kms from the Day Lodge (yurt).

# 15 Lake Tahoe Region
# East Shore-Nevada

## AREA 14. SPOONER LAKE CROSS COUNTRY SKI AREA

### Summary

Any ski program developed by an elite skier who is also an educator, as is Max Jones, will likely be outstanding. This is how it is at Spooner Lake. The easiest trails are found around the Day Lodge, more challenging ones as you move farther away, and most challenging if you ski out as far as Marlette Lake. Every forest trail has been chosen and groomed so that you get the best possible experience. Even the ski-school area has been designed with an attention to detail beyond normal commercial consideration. Spooner Lake, nestled at the junction of Highways 50 and 28 in Nevada, offers the highest level of challenge and support for the skier's potential. It's a gem.

### How to get there

*From Reno* take Hwy. 395 south through Carson City to Hwy. 50. Head west on 50, climbing to the junction with Hwy. 28. Turn right on 28 toward Incline Village and within 0.5 mile look for the entrance to Spooner Lake Cross Country Ski Area on your right. *From South Lake Tahoe* take Hwy. 50 north for 12 miles along Tahoe's east shore to the same junction with Hwy. 28. Turn left and continue as described above. *From Tahoe City* follow Hwy. 28 along Tahoe's north shore through Incline Village. Drive 11 miles south of Incline Village on 28, and look for a small CROSS-COUNTRY SKIING sign on your right. Soon after this

Dimitri Barton

*Ski in to enjoy Spooner Lake's hand-hewn cabins*

sign, turn left into Spooner Lake State Park and follow signs to the ski area. (Also note bus service in "At a Glance.")

## Description of area

This unique area is one of only two included in this book that are located outside California. (Diamond Peak, Area 13, is the other.) I've included it because of its proximity to California and because it is one of the most natural areas you'll find anywhere. The trails are not great wide swathes carved from the forest to create a ski area; they are old logging trails and routes across open meadows. With 65 kms of groomed trails meandering over 9,000 acres, though off the beaten track, Spooner Lake is not a small area.

The two trail systems are **Meadow Trails** (20 kms) and **High Country Trails** (45 kms). Of course Meadow offers easier terrain with trails all close to the Day Lodge. High Country includes intermediate and more challenging trails. The piece (*randonnée*) de resistance is undoubtedly the 18.4-km **Carson Range Trail**, of which Max Jones, designer of this steep downhill route, says, "This is the coolest, most challenging groomed trail you will ever ski—ever!" (He was a downhill racer before switching to cross-country racing.) To get there you have to ski a long way out to Marlette Lake at 7,823 feet, and over the spine of a snow-laden ridge overlooking Hobart Reservoir.

At Spooner Lake you'll see those noisy nutcrackers named after Clark, of the Lewis and Clark expedition; and you'll hear—even if you don't see—the scarlet grosbeaks that feed in the upper evergreen canopy. There's a precocious blue grouse that may demand a food-toll as you pass; and as the snow recedes the ferocious goshawk will move into the forest to breed. Spooner Lake is a hidden gem among Nordic ski areas. If you ski the milky opalescence of the Carson Range Trail, when you reach the return route called Super "G," you'll face the fire in this opal.

Other attractions of Spooner Lake Cross Country Ski Area include the unique wilderness cabins, named Wildcat and Spooner Lake. You can ski in to these extremely cozy, hand-hewn cabins designed and built by Max and his friends. The craftsmanship in their construction is matched only by the absolute privacy these cabins offer. In summer the ski area becomes a mountain-bike mecca; Max is a veteran champion at this sport also, and the cabins are once again available for rent to hikers and bikers.

## Where to stay and eat

The **Wildcat and Spooner Lake Cabins**, designed and built to entice skiers into the forest, are my first choice in lodging here. Either you carry in your supplies or they can be brought in for you. Two good hotels I can recommend are **The Ormsby** in Carson City, (775) 882-1890, and **The Hyatt Regency** at Incline Village, (775) 832-1234. The Ormsby is an old casino converted to a hotel with 200 rooms. Double-occupancy prices range from $49 for rooms to $75 for suites. They have a swimming pool, a 24-hour buffet/coffee shop, and a good in-house restaurant. The Hyatt Regency with 458 rooms offers double-occupancy room rates from $145 to $395. Three in-house dining rooms include the elegant **Lone Eagle Grill**. If The Hyatt sounds expensive don't be put off! Children under 18 years are free and if you surf their Web site (www.hyatttahoe.com), you'll find great deals—even rates as low as The Ormsby in Carson City. The Hyatt Regency manages a large number of timeshare cottages in the area, (775) 832-0220.

## *Designed by Max Jones, Expert Skier*

In 1980 when I was managing Clair Tappaan Lodge at Norden and directing its ski school, a new athlete appeared on the scene. The Lake Tahoe Region—particularly around Truckee—attracts elite athletes the way Boulder does. One draw is the climate: good predictable alpine weather, a fairly high altitude, and snow—lots of snow. (Our biggest season was in '81 when we had 841 inches.) Anyway, this new athlete, training throughout the fall for upcoming cross-country ski races, was seen roller-skiing on the local highways. His workout frequently took him along Hwy. 89 and onto Old Route 40, which climbs steeply for 4 miles from Donner Lake up to Donner Pass. These were my roller-skiing routes and until then I'd seen no one else training on them. And this fellow was good; his technique reminded me of Lyle Nelson who—four times an Olympian—was our most outstanding local athlete. That winter Max Jones would make his mark skiing the tracks and winning most of the races.

In February 1999 I went skiing with Max, meeting him at his Day Lodge yurt, the base for his cross-country skiing operation at Spooner Lake. Besides being an accomplished skier, Max is an innovative entrepreneur. Spooner Lake State Park has an outdoor cooking range here which—come winter—becomes the central heat source for the large yurt. Max and his wife, Patti McMullen (also a good skier), have chosen a beautiful area—clear of town and traffic yet easy to reach—and convinced the Nevada State Parks and the US Forest Service to let them set up an outstanding Nordic program for the skiing public.

Because Max and Patti own none of the land on which they operate, their risk has been a big one. Even the superb log cabins they've designed and built must to be dismantled if the Forest Service decrees it. But with great Nordic spirit these two have invested their lives, creating a recreation center with winter and summer programs of cross-country skiing, mountain biking, hiking, and bird watching.

Max and Patti's results after 15 years of persistent effort are impressive and even daring. Spooner Lake's program blends thoughtfully designed trails, catering to every level of skier and biker, with top-class coaching for beginning, improving, and more competent racers. Max and Patti provide a venue for local high school teams as well as citizen racers. An example of good design is in the basic teaching area for beginners. While Max has an open space on a downhill slope that levels out as you'll find in most programs, he has incorporated a trail entering the ski-school area from the top. You have to negotiate a downhill turn while still on this trail to access the ski school. So you must make a downhill turn where it's needed, rather than where it's easy on open ground.

Max gave me a skating clinic that was extremely helpful as we skated uphill on a trail toward one of the cabins. Though it wasn't steep yet, it seemed a harsh climb; my lack of altitude fitness was holding us back. After a breather, my improvement was a matter of using the hip rotation that generates the most efficient forward drive. It's too complex to adequately describe here; until you're skiing you'll have to take my word: once you get this action going your body weight offers less resistance and forward propulsion becomes transitional glide. Working together on this subtle technique, we both recalled the almost mechanical fluency—a continuum of drive, rhythm, and even uphill glide—with which Lyle Nelson used to ski. Lyle is now President of the US Biathlon Association. ❊

*Max Jones skating above Lake Tahoe*

Larry Prosor

# Area 15—At a Glance

## Camp Richardson Resort Cross Country Ski & Snowshoe Center
Box 9028, South Lake Tahoe, CA 96158
(530) 542-6584 *camp richardson . com*

### Distances From
Reno—80 mi.          Sacramento—65 mi.          Kirkwood—60 mi.
Tahoe City—31 mi.    South Lake Tahoe—2 mi.

### Elevation, Facilities, & Hours:
At Day Lodge—6,240' (little increase on cross-country terrain)
Groomed—35 kms (No dogs on groomed trails)
Ungroomed Lake Tahoe shoreline skiing (Dogs allowed)
Snowshoeing          Horse-drawn sleigh rides
Pulk sleds           Hours—9 A.M.-4 P.M.

### Passes & Rental Prices (free trail pass for children 10-)

|                        | Adult | Child |
|------------------------|-------|-------|
| Trail pass             | $10   | $10   |
| Skis, boots, & poles   | $15   | $9    |
| Snowshoes              | $15   | $9    |
| Pulk sled              | $10   | -     |
| Sleigh rides (reservation only, call (530) 541-3113) | | |
|                        | $15   | -     |

### Ski School
No major feature here—helpful demonstration before setting out. *lift first pass us*

*Queen midwk 50 55 cont*

### Lodging & Food
Camp Richardson Hotel (29 hotel rooms) from $45 to $95; The Beachside
Inn (7 rooms); many lakeside cabins for 2-8 persons; lakeside condo, (800)
544-1801. Restaurants include the Beacon Bar & Grill, The Emerald Bay Cafe
& Deli (breakfast and lunch), and The Fresh Ketch (10 minutes away by car)
in Tahoe Keys Marina.
**Winter special:** Double-occupancy room with cross-country trail pass (Sunday-
Thursday) $39.
**Shuttle:** Inquire about shuttle service between Camp Richardson and
Kirkwood.

Baldwin
1 800 526 1986

DVD

Meadows —
Q 3-189  2-149  incl
trail passes

Cove Richardson
Queen w/bath
50 midweek    cont bkfast
55 weekend    trail passes

King Brightside
$80 king        pkg
Queen 75  Bkfast 50    Jan Jan
King 85              5 - 9  10  10th

14 days cancel    3P election   11 A election
                  1d    412 00
Leo

# 16   Lake Tahoe Region

# South Shore

## AREA 15. CAMP RICHARDSON RESORT CROSS COUNTRY SKI & SNOWSHOE CENTER

### Summary

Seventy-five years old and recognized for its inexpensive, quality year-round operation, Camp Richardson borders Lake Tahoe and sits astride Hwy. 89 like a small self-contained town. Here, you can either ski along the lakeshore with your dog for free or, across the road, ski under Jeffrey pine toward Fallen Leaf Lake on the ski center's groomed trails. The trails though narrow are well groomed for striding and skating. This is a low-key cross-country area, with easy terrain that's ideal for the beginning skier. For modest fees Camp Richardson offers skiing, snowshoeing, sledding, and sleigh rides. Equipment rentals and beginner lessons are also available. Accommodations, a general store, and restaurants (including a cafe) are all nearby.

### How to get there

*From Reno* head south on Hwy. 395, and then take Hwy. 50 (as you also will when driving *from Sacramento*) to South Lake Tahoe. At the junction of Hwy. 89, head north up the lake's west shore. In 2 miles you will find the Camp Richardson Hotel on your right and the Mountain Sports Center on your left. *From Tahoe City* drive 31 miles south on Hwy. 89 to the Camp Richardson Hotel on your left (2 miles short of the Hwy. 50 junction in South Lake Tahoe).

*Camp Richardson Hotel*

In winter, particularly after major snowstorms, this very winding section of Hwy. 89 is hazardous and often closed for avalanche control. If it's closed (check with CalTrans to find out), drive right around the lake on Highways 28 and 50 to get there.

## Description of area

Each conveniently color-coded trail makes a loop, so that you can always find your position using the map provided here. On easy terrain, no steep climbs or downhills confront the beginner. The trails wind through a forest of Jeffrey pine, a few old Douglas-fir, and cypress. But the meadows boast small stands of aspen trees with pallid, susurrant leaves. In Chaucer's *Troilus*, when Creseyde first saw this prince, "She trembled like an aspen leaf."

The groomed trails aren't wide because Camp Richardson Resort is operated under permit from the US Forest Service, and all trails must be maintained to their specifications. With room for just one striding track beside the skating lane, there's still no sense of crowding on these trails because skiers tend to go one way. On 35 kms of groomed trails, the whole skiing and snowshoeing program is ideal for the novice; you can take a lesson or safely wander off on your own. For a wonderful change of pace, there's the horse-drawn sleigh with its own trail. Children love it.

## Where to stay and eat

**Camp Richardson Resort**, (800) 544-1801, known locally as Camp "Rich," has a wide range of year-round accommodations: an historic hotel (bearing the resort's name) with 29 rooms and many lakefront cabins; the Beachside Inn with 7 rooms; and a lakefront condo. The Winter Special, your best deal available Sunday-Thursday, provides a double-occupancy room and trail pass for $39. Other double-occupancy winter rates range from $45 to $95.

Dining is excellent at the camp's own **Beacon Bar & Grill**, in a delightful room overlooking Lake Tahoe. **The Fresh Ketch** in the Tahoe Keys Marina (owned by Camp Richardson) is also good. **The Emerald Bay Cafe & Deli** next door to the main hotel serves breakfast or lunch. For a robust breakfast alternative, I recommend driving to **The Red Hut Cafe** on South Lake Tahoe Blvd. for their scrumptious Eggs Benedict.

## *A Birding Ramble on Skis*

It's very pleasant to amble on touring skis in mid-March beside the shore of Lake Tahoe. Along the littoral mallard ducks and Canada geese are feeding and paddling about, while offshore I spot a female American merganser. This diving duck catches small fish and lives on the lake year-round, but her partner, the startlingly handsome black-and-white drake with his long scarlet bill, winters elsewhere. I know he's due back soon.

Around the corner from this beach is Emerald Bay, where both the osprey and the bald eagle breed. To see either of these fish-catching raptors—the osprey, plunge feet first into water and then struggle back into flight with its catch, or the eagle that doesn't plunge but snatches a fish from just below the water's surface as it passes over—is an impressive sight. Visualizing these birds while skiing this shoreline fills me with anticipatory pleasure.

After lunch I visit with John Dunn and Matt Bishop in the Cross Country Ski Center, across Hwy. 89 just opposite the camp's hotel. I see that all their ski equipment is Alpina, and that they have a large number of snowshoes for rent. I pick up a map and set off into the forest on my skating skis, heading toward Fallen Leaf Lake. All the color-coded routes are also marked in kilometers. You cannot get lost at this area and, because of the dispersion of the trees, you can actually see where you are going, which isn't often the case in a forest setting.

This is a forest of Jeffrey pines, and I love the way they do not cling too close together. The pines' coarse roots—in this nitrogen-deficient soil—rely on a fungicidal growth system

113

Gary Silva

*Skiing Tahoe's lakeshore*

needing plenty of space and accounting for the spread. This constraint of nature, which can be seen as a refinement, allows me an open view. I enjoy this openness, not least because I get to view the local birds that thrive in these less densely forested byways.

Because bird watching has been as rewarding as skiing in my life, when I find myself surrounded by interesting birds on skis I'm in Paradise. (Paradise, by the way, is wherever I am without anxiety.) Clark's nutcrackers call to each other but none come into view. They are lovely soft-gray birds with vivid black-and-white wings. I hear a nuthatch go "beep, beep, beep," sounding just like a truck signals when it's backing up. Then I hear a woodpecker's drilling, very loudly, as I stop to admire a group of aspens in an open meadow.

The woodpecker stops its machine-gun drilling and lets out a raucous yell, "Wuck-a-wuck-a-wuck," which suggests to me it may be flying. Then I see him, big as a crow, come flapping and gliding over the aspens and across the meadow. He heads toward and literally collides with a grand old pine with a trunk "four feet thick at the base." Since he hit the tree hard, I wonder if he hasn't just learned about "its being, without seeming," Walt Whitman's "Lesson of a Tree." He's the biggest of them all. I can tell from his vivid red patch that comes all the way from his crested forehead to his massive beak that he is a male pileated (crested) woodpecker.

This evening I have a superb dinner with my hosts at their Beacon Bar & Grill. Heidi Dunn is too full to eat her second Alaskan crab leg, so I get to eat it with my filet mignon; an American classic—surf n' turf. I tell them Camp Richardson is just a wonderful place for a quiet walk in the woods on skis, rather than a place to rush around as I so often do on racing skis. ❋

# Area 16—At a Glance

### Sorensen's Hope Valley Cross Country Ski Center
Sorensen's Resort, 14255 Hwy. 88, Hope Valley, CA 96120
Lodging at Sorensen's (800) 423-9949    (530) 694-2203
Hope Valley Cross Country skiing & snowshoeing information
(530) 694-2266

### Distance From
Sacramento—110 mi.    Reno—65 mi.    Tahoe City—45 mi.
S. Lake Tahoe—20 mi.

### Nearest Airport
Reno International—65 miles.

### Elevation, Facilities, & Hours
Trails—7,000-8,300'        Ungroomed trails—100 kms
Wilderness telemarking    Moonlight tours
Dogs allowed              Snowshoeing
Cafe hours —9 A.M.-5 P.M. (also for rental equipment)

### Rental Prices

|                    | Light | Mid-weight | Backcountry | Child's |
|--------------------|-------|------------|-------------|---------|
| Touring equipment  | $12   | $14        | $16         | $8      |
| Snowshoes          | $12   |            |             |         |
| Snowboards         | $20   |            |             |         |

### Ski Lessons
Beginning $22, intermediate or telemark $22; Adventure lesson (with mini-tour) $45, Adventure tour (full 3-hr.) $50.

### Ski Packages

|                 | Adult | Child | Telemark |
|-----------------|-------|-------|----------|
| Rental & lesson | $30   | $20   | $32      |

For other guided tours and programs, call (530) 694-2266 for information.

### The Husky Express
Dogsled teams mush over Hope Valley snowfields—advanced reservations only (775) 782-3047.

### Lodging & Food
A year-round resort designed like a Norwegian log village, Sorensen's has 3 complete houses for up to 6 people each (one dog friendly), ranging from $195 to $450. Many cabins offer various options for 1 to 6 people (no phone or TV) from $180 to $275. The main lodge has a dining room serving breakfast, lunch, & dinner. A public phone is conveniently located outside the main lodge. The Cross Country Ski Center (with cafe/general store) is 300 yds. east of Sorensen's on Hwy. 88.

# 17  SOUTH of LAKE TAHOE

# HOPE VALLEY

## AREA 16. SORENSEN'S HOPE VALLEY
## CROSS COUNTRY SKI CENTER

### Summary

Sorensen's is a year-round resort, which looks like a Norwegian wilderness village, at the hub of 25,000 acres of Eldorado National Forest. Every hand-built log cabin is situated so that you walk downhill from it to the "Village Center," or administrative lodge and dining room. The cross-country skiing and snowshoeing programs are run from the Hope Valley Outdoor Center, just 300 yards down the road. The Kirkwood ski areas are 14 miles west; many people skiing there stay at Sorensen's. The Hope Valley skiing operation is unique because it covers a wide area of forest and flat, open ground with 100 kms of trails but no machine grooming. All the teaching and touring is for backcountry conditions, and Nina Thor, a veteran Norwegian skier, is a master at teaching for them. Another unique feature is the Alaskan-style adventure of mushing across snowfields on a sled pulled by 10 or 12 huskies. The experts for this event are Dotty Dennis and Dave Beck. Dave also coaches advanced, wilderness Nordic skiing techniques.

### How to get there

*From Reno* drive 45 miles south on Hwy. 395 toward Minden. One mile short of Minden, continue south on Hwy. 88. In 20 miles Sorensen's will be on your

*The Norwegian-style village of log cabins at Sorensen's Resort blends indoor comfort with outdoor adventure*

Renee Lynn/Sorensen's Resort

left. (There's no gas available on Hwy. 88. One mile beyond the Hwy. 395 junction with Hwy. 88, in Minden, is the best buy in Nevada.) *From South Lake Tahoe* drive 20 miles south on Hwy. 89 to the junction with Hwy. 88. Turn left on 88, and Sorensen's will soon appear on your right.

## Description of area

With its blend of forest trails, mountain slopes, and wide, open meadows, this is a diverse area. Since John and Patti Brissenden, the owners of Sorensen's, are much involved in ecological issues, none of their recreational skiing territory is groomed. Here, you'll discover an elemental Nordic skiing and snowshoeing program offered by their Hope Valley Cross Country Ski Center, with an outstanding teacher and guide, Nina Thor. Besides rentals and tours, basic skiing lessons are taught here. You can either ski or snowshoe a comfortable 4 or 5 kilometers to the ski center, or drive there and park in one of several designated off-road lots.

Romantics will love the adventure offered by **The Husky Express**. Hope Valley meadows constitute a local tundra that is perfect for the teams of huskies Dotty Dennis and Dave Beck bring to the party. Ten dogs can pull a cargo of 375 lbs, with their musher cadging a lift on the sled's rear runners. Dave Beck, who not only mushes but is a veteran Nordic/Alpine instructor, offers coaching and a guide service by appointment with a two-student minimum, (775) 782-3047.

## Where to stay and eat

The treat at **Sorensen's** (a no-smoking resort) is staying in one of their many comfortable and quaint log cabins. They are extremely cozy with log fires, cooking ranges, showers—every convenience except, of course, telephones and TV. With ample wood stacked on your cabin porch, the fireplace has paper, kindling, and logs waiting for you to put a match to them. Cabins sleep from 1 to 6 people, and winter prices range from a midweek, non-holiday rate for double occupancy of $180 to $225 for four people. Prices are higher on weekends and highest during special-event weekends. **The Norway House** is the showcase of the property; you can't help noticing it if you drive by Sorensen's. A replica of a 13th century Norwegian home, it accommodates six people. The winter rate for this classic lodging may be from $195 to $450, depending on the time of week and season. The resort's **Cafe/Restaurant** features a very inviting and intimate dining room, a superior menu (Roast duck for me!), and a good chef. Breakfast, lunch, and dinner are served. The **Hope Valley Outdoor Center Cafe** is 300 yards down the road.

## _Mushing with Dogs_

All the cabins here have interesting names. I'm in the one called "'Snowshoe' Thompson" after the emigrant Norwegian, John Thorenson, a skier in the 1850s who became a living legend as the Sierra's first winter mailman. As I'm writing this in my Snowshoe snuggery there's a knock on the door, so I put down my pen to see who's there. A trim-looking woman, as anxious not to disturb as to meet me, introduces herself as "Nina Thor, Ski Instructor." She's heard that I'm writing this book on Nordic skiing. Inviting her in for a cup of tea, I can see and hear that Nina is Norwegian to the core. Since I've skied the Telemark Region and raced several times in the _Holmenkolen Marchen_, the famous 42-km citizen race held just outside Oslo every year, Nina and I have plenty in common besides a love of teaching skiing.

In the morning we have breakfast together and I meet her skiing companion, the wolf-husky named "Yoik." _Yoik_, by the way, is the old Lappish word for the Laplanders' style of yodeling. Though Yoik can't yodel, when the three of us go skiing he doesn't need skis and has a much better time of it than we do.

The snow is so boilerplate hard after yesterday's sun and last night's deep freeze that it's hard to enjoy. It needs a couple hours' sun to loosen up the crust. Before we abandon skis, I've had time to see the blend of attack and smoothness inherent in Nina's skiing. If you ski with Nina she'll coach

*Ski instructor Nina Thor is watched by her wolf-husky, Yoik*

rather than teach. She'll encourage you to copy her "natural form," skiing the true Norwegian way on ungroomed snow. Since the snow may be loose and deep or crusty, you get an experience quite different from that of skiing on groomed snow.

Nina drives me up the road to what I now call the Hope Valley tundra; with a snowy owl sitting on a hummock this could be Alaska. Here, the Husky Express meets its clients, some of whom reach Hope Valley from the casinos in stretch limos. These clients get a fresh air and exercise break from their indoor recreation without exerting themselves. We're in luck because Dotty Dennis and Dave Beck arrived just ahead of us with two teams of huskies. They're packing their casino cargo into warm furs before whisking them away over the snow. While I've been acquainted with Dave Beck for 20 years, I've not seen him since I left the Sierra. His reputation as a Nordic/Alpine guide is well established, and he published a book on backcountry skiing some time ago.

By driving down the valley in Nina's car, we catch up with Dave's team. Dave takes his clients for a long run down the valley and back. When the huskies get a break, I hack my way out without skis to get some photos of them. Then away he goes on the return run with a dad and two children, I think. It's hard to tell; they're so well wrapped up. But his huskies are having a marvelous time as they rush over the snow, giving voice like Gabriel's hounds, an insanely beautiful sound that stays in the air long after they've gone. ❄

*The Husky Express whisks guests across the Hope Valley tundra*

# Area 17—At a Glance

## Caples Lake Resort

Box 88, Kirkwood, CA 95646
phone (209) 258-8888    fax (209) 258-8898
www.caples.com            caples@volcano.net
*capleslakeresort.com*

## Distance From

San Francisco—190 mi.   Sacramento—115 mi.   Stockton—100 mi.
Reno—80 mi.               Jackson—60 mi.
South Lake Tahoe—30 mi.

## Elevation & Facilities

At lakeside resort—7,800′. Skiing/Snowshoeing is ungroomed & off-track. Kirkwood Cross Country Ski Area and Downhill Ski Area are respectively 1 mile and 1.5 miles east.

## Rental Prices

**Snowshoes:** $15. Other downhill/cross-country skiing equipment can be rented at Kirkwood (see prices for Area 18). No trail fees for snowshoeing/skiing on Emigrant Trail circling Caples Lake.

## Lodging & Food

Resort has 9 housekeeping cabins with prices ranging $90-$270 per night for 2-6 people. There are 9 B and B rooms in the main lodge, ranging $50-$110 per night. Main lodge has a big combined lounge/dining room. Caples Lake Dining Room serves the best dinner anywhere on Hwy. 88; make reservations. Closed Tuesdays.
**Entrees:** Ranging $5.95 (Child)-$25.95, served with homemade soup or salad, fresh vegetables, plus potatoes or rice unless you're eating pasta. Try— Grilled New York Steak & Scampi; Vegetable Casserole; Chicken Marsala; Fresh Fish; Charbroiled Chicken Breast; and Nightly Specials. Children's entrees are 50% off the same menu. 5 dessert choices and a good wine list.

# 18 SouTh of LAkE TAHOE
# CARSON PASS
# & KiRkwood

## AREA 17. CAPLES LAKE RESORT

### Setting

Driving west over Carson Pass you find yourself in a far more rugged environ-ment than what you found in Hope Valley. Now in a truly alpine setting, you see snow piled much higher at the roadside, there are pullouts for slower vehi-cles, and the road's sweeping curves conform to the mountains' rugged tailor-ing. A large lake is situated on your left, and carved out of the snow berm is the entrance to Caples Lake Resort.

### How to get there

Drive 13 miles west of Sorensen's (Area 16), or 1.5 miles east of the main entrance of Kirkwood (Area 18). Either way, you're on Hwy. 88.

### Description of area

Caples Lake Resort is a four-season operation on the Mormon Emigrant Trail. It offers a wide range of activities: downhill and cross-country skiing (at Kirkwood), hiking, snowshoeing, biking, sailing, kayaking, canoeing, fly-fish-

*Ideally situated to host skiers, Caples Lake Resort is noted for its fine food*

ing, horseback riding, and birding. The lake at an elevation of 7,800 feet comes up to the resort's main lodge. The housekeeping cabins and lodge rooms are pleasing and the food is excellent.

## *Purgatory and Redemption, Desert and Snow*

When I ski at Kirkwood my best accommodation is at John Voss's Caples Lake Resort. There's no all-night grooming going on here. And I've read *Voss*, the novel by the acclaimed Australian author, Patrick White. When I first met John we were standing in the snow while he pointed out my lodging. I asked him if he knew his namesake in this novel set in a harsh Australian desert. It's a story about a scientific expedition on which there's the threat of depravity due to continual deprivation. Voss is one of the scientists—one who is obsessed with his own survival.

Many years ago I led a group of scientists to the Tanami Desert in Australia's Northern Territory. This survey expedition had the goal of developing a Bouget Anomaly, a chart to measure variations in the earth's gravity. One mathematician behaved just like Patrick White's Voss, and conditions were so purgatorially hot that we lived like Dante's shades in that desert. The pilots who flew our helicopters knew all about redemption, because they could take leave breaks to ski 2,000 miles away at Falls Creek. I tell John this story and how furious some well-respected American book critics were when a writer they'd never heard of from "Down Under" was awarded the Nobel Prize for Literature. "It Voss too much for them," I say. And John confesses that he only bought the book because it had his name on it. ❆

*World Masters Champion in four events, Debbi Waldear of Kirkwood Cross Country*

# Area 18—At a Glance

## Kirkwood Cross Country

Box 1, Kirkwood, CA 64695
Resort (209) 258-6000
Cross Country Skiing Center (209) 258-7248
www.skikirkwood.com

## Distance From

Bay Area—190 mi.          Sacramento—115 mi.          Reno—81 mi.
South Lake Tahoe—31 mi.

## Nearest Airport

Reno International—80 miles.

## Elevation, Facilities, & Hours

Trails—7,800-9,000'          Groomed—80 kms
Telemark—Lift-served at adjacent Downhill area          Dogs—20 kms
Snowshoeing          Pulk sleds          Hours—9 A.M.-5 P.M.

## Passes & Rental Prices (free trail pass for children 6-)

|  | Adults | Jr./Sr. (13-18/60+) | Child (7-12) |
|---|---|---|---|
| Trail pass | $15 | $11 | $5 |
| Skis, boots, & poles |  |  |  |
| track | $15 | $15 | $9 |
| skating | $20 | - | - |
| backcountry | $20 | - | - |
| telemark | $25 | - | - |
| Snowshoes | $12 | - | - |
| Pulk sled | $12 | - | - |

## Ski School

|  | Adults | Jr. /Sr. | Child |
|---|---|---|---|
| Beginner's Package (includes trail pass & equipment) |  |  |  |
| track | $35 | $30 | $20 |
| skating | $40 | $35 | $25 |

Special Lessons: Telemark with half-day lift ticket (weekends only) $50.
Stop & Turn with trail pass (weekends only) $25; private lesson $25 per hour.

## Lodging & Food

Call Kirkwood Lodging Services (800) 967-7500 for full details on the following accommodations: The Lodge at Kirkwood (luxury units), Sun Meadows, The Meadows, Edelweiss & Thimblewood, Base Camp. All are close to Meadows Trail System. Prices range from $129 (double occupancy) to $465 for up to 8 guests. Kirkwood Resort has numerous restaurants: near Cross Country Ski Center is the Old Kirkwood Inn (est. 1864) with good food. Caples Lake Resort has good lodging and gourmet food (1 mile east of center on Hwy. 88).

# AREA 18. KIRKWOOD CROSS COUNTRY

## Summary

Rising from 7,800 feet, this Nordic ski area is high and gets more snow than most. The easiest of three trail systems is Kirkwood Meadow, offering novice skiers 10 kms of groomed trail over gentle terrain. With varied terrain and some spectacular scenery, Caples Creek Trail System is for more advanced skiers. If you're a naturalist, the best route takes you past a beaver pond on your way downhill to Caples Meadow. The Schneider Trail System is the most challenging one. You can ski this area from the Schneider parking lot, 3 miles east of Kirkwood. This system leads you up into Kirkwood's high country and delivers spectacular views. You'll find a warming hut where you need it on the higher ground.

## How to get there

*From Sacramento or South Lake Tahoe* take Hwy. 50 to the junction of Hwy. 89 in Meyers. Head south on 89 over Luther Pass to Picketts Junction and turn right (west) onto Hwy. 88. Drive 14 miles on 88 over Carson Pass to Kirkwood Cross Country, just past Caples Lake Resort on the right. *From Reno* take Hwy. 395 south to the junction of Hwy. 88 (1 mile short of Minden) and continue on 88 for 34 miles to Kirkwood.

## Description of area

Two cross-country ski areas in California bear the imprint of Olympic biathlete Glenn Jobe's hand and both are outstanding. Glenn's first effort was here at Kirkwood and the other was Tahoe Donner (Area 8). He designed and built Kirkwood Cross Country and later sold it to the Kirkwood Resort. Debbi Waldear, a former alpine ski instructor, came to Kirkwood 20 years ago to train with Glenn. After a swift rise through racing-community ranks, Debbi was soon the top skier in the Far West. In 1984 she joined the Rossignol Team. When Glenn sold Kirkwood, Debbi replaced him as director. She maintains the high standards for which this area has become well known.

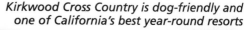

*Kirkwood Cross Country is dog-friendly and one of California's best year-round resorts*

The warmly robust atmosphere at Kirkwood starts at the Day Lodge, a converted country house with a friendly staff, a comprehensive rental shop (Rossignol skis rule here), and a handy snack bar. The 80 kms of well-groomed trails, which compose three trail systems, give each skier (of whatever level) the opportunity to roam a wide range and variety of terrain. Since Debbi Waldear breeds llamas and dogs, it isn't surprising that Kirkwood Cross Country is a dog-friendly ski center. The High Trail leading from the lodge is a designated route for dogs.

Beginners, children, and less-fit skiers should start out on the **Kirkwood Meadow** 10-km loop, beginning across the road from the Day Lodge, because of its easy terrain and proximity to the lodge. (This area can also be accessed from its south end behind Kirkwood's Sun Meadows condominiums.) You'll find the Cornice Cafe as well as a warming hut at the south end of the meadow. Views are spectacular, including that of Round Top Peak—at 10,380 feet the highest mountain in the region. Yet, the great Red Cliffs bordering the meadow's east side and the massive mountain background to the south and west are visually most impressive.

**Caples Creek** is the most varied trail system and, if you're a naturalist, the one to head for. Skiing down the long, rolling descent to Caples Meadow—following the winding creek, passing a beaver pond—you may meet a great blue heron or even a great-horned owl. Start out from the lodge on the Caples Creek Trail, which joins Beaver Pond.

With its own trailhead parking lot 2.5 miles east of the Day Lodge, the **Schneider Trail System** is an elaborate network north of Hwy. 88. It provides access to the high country where the best views are. For the classic tour take Juniper and Aspen trails uphill to the Outpost Trail, along which you'll head to the old Schneider Cow Camp barn. After lunch at the nearby warming hut, you can continue climbing on the Sierra Vista Trail to Coyote Pass. From this high vantage you can look down to Caples Lake and the Day Lodge, as well as across the valley to Carson Spur. This range of peaks hosts the many downhill trails of Kirkwood Alpine Ski Area.

## Where to stay and eat

Just 0.5 mile west of the cross-country center is the entrance to Kirkwood on your left. Turn left and follow the west side of Kirkwood Meadow another 0.5 mile to the village. Here, **Kirkwood Lodging Services**, (800) 967-7500, offer five good accommodations. Refer to "Area 18—At a Glance" for listings and a price range.

There are numerous restaurants and bars in the village: **Red Cliffs Lodge, Cornice Cafe, Timber Creek Lodge, Zak's Bar** and **Off The Wall.** Lodging packages include a Midweek Getaway with 20% savings on room rates (Sunday through Thursday except holidays). **Caples Lake Resort,** 1 mile east of Kirkwood Cross Country, has lodging and excellent food (see Area 17). For a comfortable English pub-style atmosphere, **Kirkwood Inn** (next door to the Day Lodge) offers a hearty lunch and dinner menu.

## Debbi Waldear and Cross-country Women's Racing

Though I've never skied the 22-km Echo Summit to Kirkwood cross-country race, it's a well-known classic on the California Citizen Racing calendar that's on my treat list for the year 2000. I'd like to ski it with Debbi Waldear, Director of the Kirkwood Cross Country Skiing Center, but I'm afraid she's too fast for me. Debbi, born in 1948, who supposedly retired from racing some years ago, has brought a slew of gold medals back to Kirkwood from the World Masters Championships over the past three years. Last year she won every event in her age group, returning home with four gold medals: three golds for skating and diagonal stride in the 5-to-30-km events, and another in the 4X5-km relay.

Since she came to California about 20 years ago, I've kept an eye on Debbi Waldear's career. When I first raced with her at Royal Gorge, she distinguished herself—particularly in the downhill sections. A cross-country racer gains a huge advantage by skiing fast downhill and recuperates from oxygen debt while doing so. Less-skillful downhill skiers lose time skiing cautiously on the only part of the course that's a free ride.

Soon Debbi became an elite Nordic racer, winning in 1987 the Great American Ski Chase, a series of marathon races that take place across the country. She also won the first US National Championship for 20 kms at Royal Gorge. That year the authorities decided women could actually race farther than 10 kms without fainting. Women weren't allowed to compete in an Olympic Marathon until the Los Angeles Olympics. A woman from Maine, whom the Olympic Committee would have disregarded, won it. That was Joan Benoit. Debbi Waldear, also, has realized the potential that all women athletes can achieve but weren't always welcome to. When California Proposition 9, which granted equal funding to college women's teams, became law, the tide began to turn.

Two team sports played by women in college, basketball and soccer, have become benchmark sports. Though it has college-team and national-team competition, cross-country skiing remains an individual's sport. Just to discover one's own potential calls for the highest level of self-discipline. When Debbi invited herself into the cross-country citizen-racing community, who knew where her efforts would lead? That community and all those recreational skiers who come her way at Kirkwood recognize and honor Debbi Waldear's national and world-class achievements. ❄

# Area 19—At a Glance

### Bear Valley Cross Country
Box 5120, Bear Valley, CA 95223

(209) 753-2834       www.bearvalleyxc.com       bvcc@sonnet.com

### Distances From
Reno—250 mi.       San Francisco—165 mi.       San Jose—165 mi.
Sacramento—125 mi.  Stockton—94 mi.            Angels Camp—43 mi.

### Nearest Airports
Sacramento—125 mi.   San Francisco—165 mi.

### Elevation, Facilities, & Hours

| | | |
|---|---|---|
| Trails—7,000-7,557' | Groomed—65 kms | Telemark |
| Warming huts | Snowshoeing | Kid's sledding hill |
| Pulk sleds | Moonlight skiing | Dogsled weekend |
| Ski-orienteering meetings | Hours—9 A.M.-4:30 P.M. | |

### Passes & Rental Prices (free trail pass for children 8-)

| | Adults | Jr./Sr. (13-17/60+) | Child (9-12) |
|---|---|---|---|
| Trail pass | $16 | $11 | $8 |
| **Skis, boots, & poles** | | | |
| track/skating | $15 | $15 | - |
| **Telemark** | $20 | - | - |
| **Snowshoes** | $12 | - | - |
| **Pulk sled** (by reservation) | $15 | - | - |

### Ski School

| | Adults | Child (9-12) |
|---|---|---|
| **Intro cross-country package** (includes lesson, equipment rental, and trail pass) | | |
| track | $36 | $28 |
| skating | $38 | $31 |

Group lesson (without trail pass) $15. Private lesson $35; each additional person $15. Skiing Bears (ages 4-8) lesson (weekends only) $15. Inquire about Telemark lesson.

### Lodging & Food
Bear Valley Lodge, (209) 753-2327, is a destination hotel with 51 rooms, a cathedral lounge, an excellent dining room, and a spacious bar/lounge. Rooms (double occupancy) are $90-$135. Suites range $180-$245. Tamarack Pines Inn, (209) 753-2080, is a 6-room B and B offering trailside rooms and selling trail passes. Other available accommodations: Nordic Hostel (209) 753-2834, Red Dog Lodge, Mountain Adventure Seminars (209) 753-6556, and Tamarack Resort (209) 753-2001 all with restaurant & bar. For all other Calaveras County lodgings on Highway 4, call (800) 225-3764.

# 19   NORTH of YOSEMITE
# BEAR Valley

## AREA 19. BEAR VALLEY CROSS COUNTRY

### Summary

Bear Valley offers a wonderful range of cross-country skiing, from the very flat terrain accessed at Meadow trailhead near the Cross Country Center to more advanced hilly trails. Plenty of intermediate trails head out to 7,557-foot Osborn Ridge, or farther west to Canyon Vista overlooking the North Fork of the Stanislaus River. Views south from the Dardanelles to distant Yosemite are stunning. Bear Valley's ski school is excellent and their rental equipment is all Rossignol boots and skis. The interior of the Bear Valley Lodge is one of the best in California; its spacious reception and lounge area is cathedral-like in design yet absolutely warm and relaxing. Unless you visit great timber-built hotels such as Montebello in Canada, you won't find a toastier grand fireplace.

### How to get there

*From the Bay Area* go 50 miles east on I-580 to the junction of I-5 east of Tracy, and continue north on I-5 to Stockton. Watch for repeated signs for Angels Camp and be ready to make quick route changes: first onto I-205 east, then briefly on Hwy. 99 south, and finally on Hwy. 4 east to Angels Camp. **All-weather Hwy. 4 is the only winter route to Bear Valley. Carry chains.** Watch for the Bear Valley Cross Country sign 43 miles east of Angels Camp. *From Reno* take I-80 west to the junction of I-5 in Sacramento and drive south on I-5 to Stockton. Continue through Stockton (as described above) to Bear Valley.

## Description of Area

Starting about 20 years ago, "the kid," 20-year-old Paul Petersen, made Bear Valley his home and his mission. Today, he is President of Bear Valley Cross Country. On 3,000 acres Paul has created one of the best Nordic skiing areas in North America. For 65 kms twin striding tracks with a broad skating lane wend through forest over hill and dale. It all starts at the Bear Valley Cross Country Center on Highway 4. The Day Lodge and Ski Shop are located on the north side of the road, while the roadside trailhead directly opposite leads into a huge meadow on the south side.

At the west end of the trail system is Tamarack Pines Inn. If you're a guest you can buy your trail pass here and ski directly onto the tracks. At the east end of the system (3 miles after crossing Bloods Creek on Hwy. 4) is Bear Valley Ski Company's Alpine operation. From the warming hut at 7,235-foot Scenic Vista, there are magnificent views across the North Fork of the Stanislaus River to the Dardanelles. You can see 11,570-foot Leavitt Peak and 10,808-foot Relief Peak. To top it all you can look south and—with an eagle's eye—see Yosemite almost 30 miles away.

The trailside cafe is only 1 km from Meadow trailhead, and there are warming huts farther east and west for the chilled or weary. There's a hill for kids to go sledding and pulk sleds for parents to tow their small children while skiing. Paul Petersen has worked with Rossignol to develop shorter-than-standard skis and better boots for the Bear Valley rental program. This more manageable and comfortable equipment has enabled beginners to turn and stop with greater ease. Since Bear Valley is a year-round resort, the comprehensive rental and retail store caters not only to skiers. In summer it becomes a store for hikers, canoeists, kayakers, and bikers.

*Besides being well known for his skiing and teaching, Paul Petersen is comfortable on snowshoes, too*

## Where to stay and eat

**Bear Valley Lodge** is my first choice in accommodations for its combinations of comfort with elegance and good food with good service, (209) 753-2327. I also like the much smaller **Tamarack Pines Inn** (B and B), which is small, friendly, and warm, (209) 753-2080. **Bear Valley Real Estate** handles vacation homes and condo rentals, (209) 753-2334. For offering sleeping-bag accommodation many free-heel skiers will find the **Nordic Hostel** useful, (209) 753-2834. **Tamarack Resort** is an historic lodge with restaurant and bar, (209) 753-2001. **Red Dog Lodge** has dormitory-style accommodations with breakfast, (209) 753-2344. The best source for all other Highway 4 accommodation is **Calaveras County Lodging**, (800) 225-3764. Finally, an extension of the Bear Valley Lodge called "the Village" is a place where you can get snacks, a cappuccino, breakfast, or lunch.

## *A Romp at Bear Valley*

"Imperfect as the wind" wrote Wordsworth, and so it certainly was today. Forty cross-country skiers, all a bit mad, met just after April Fool's Day at Bear Valley to ski a race despite a blizzard. We tried to start at 9 A.M. but were delayed by a temperature change that dropped the barometer a sharp 8° below freezing, while the imperfect wind added a serious chill factor to the safety equation. It was snowing hard and the wind not only blew swirling, gritty snow into our eyes, it completely obliterated the track for the start of our event, "Tom's Race."

This classic-style 10-km race is the last event of the cross-country ski season at Bear Valley. It commemorates the life of a popular Bear Valley skier, Tom Reichle, whose life was struck down by a drunk motorist. For a while it looked as though the race would have to be called off because the wind had no regard for our plans. We were to ski a course over open terrain, giving us the best views. But open terrain means open to the wind as well. The weather had literally wiped out our race course.

However, Paul Petersen is of Norwegian stock and not inclined to defer to a weather god's conniption fit. Paul ignors Thor but acknowledges wise Odin. He asks all skiers to wait one hour in the Day Lodge while he sets a new and safer course, with tracks winding entirely through the forest so that we'll be out of the wind. When it's ready we all huddle out to the start line on the meadow; then away we go, laughing and squinting into the sleetlike, stinging snow.

In these conditions the cold, sharp snow crystals allow little glide and the tracks quickly fill with loose snow. The grip wax under the ski's midsection won't bond well to give the necessary grip for a good stride. Knowing this, even some of the experienced skiers have chosen nonwax skis with a configuration underfoot that guarantee a bond. Yet what they gain on grip they lose on glide. I'm on waxed skis because Paul has let me try out his Rossi' racing skis. He even applied a good glide wax the night before, letting me apply the grip wax minutes before the race when I'll know best what's needed. With this sudden temperature change, dropping to 8° below freezing in the past hour, I'd have been on the wrong wax if I'd chosen sooner. So now I'm on a hard blue wax.

The few hot young racers who have shown up shoot off from the start. Their skis are like arrows attached to them—their bodies are the bows. They disappear into the blizzard. At 2 kms I determine my position in the race; I'm in 13th place just behind a woman, and we two are widely separated from those ahead and those behind. We are well into the forest and it's as though we are skiing a pas de deux, where she's setting the tempo. I must pass her before we get to a steep downhill section ahead; otherwise, being heavier I'm bound to run into her.

The tracks are filling with snow and snow swirls around us, making visibility difficult. I pass my partner, and before the downhill levels off there's a curve in the track that requires some weight shifting on my ski edges. But there is no set track to hold my skis in line; it's entirely filled in. My left ski starts wandering, right in the middle of the curve. Losing control of it, I plant my right pole firmly for some support while moving fast. My balance recovered, I have to give the right pole a good yank to break it free.

It breaks free all right, flying through the air ahead of me as I crash into the deep, soft snow beside the track. No harm's done; my partner is far enough behind not to be caught up in my collapse, and she's nimble enough to ski around me. But struggling to my feet, I find my right pole's handle is still strapped to my hand. The pole has snapped 8″ from the top; it was the long shaft I'd seen flying through the air. I look and soon find it, a planted metallic-blue wand.

I seize the errant shaft at the top, putting my thumb over the hollow stem so that my hand doesn't slip. It's not impossible to ski with one short pole but inconvenient for sure. Since no one has passed me during this mishap, off I go in pursuit of number 12. She looms ahead sooner than I'd hoped, which tells me she must be tiring. As I pass her she says, "That was unbelievable. Good luck."

"You too," I call to her. But I'm thinking, "Never mind luck, I need a new pole."

While I'd deliberately started out with extra-long poles for powerful pushing, now I must compensate with accurate ski-to-ski weight shifting and hip thrust. I ski like this for the next 5 kms, until I spot a lone spectator standing back to the weather at a trail junction. What catches my eye is the long length of his ski poles. I ski up to him, show him my broken pole, and say, "Please, please, lend me a pole to get through the race." Seeing my short pole, he responds immediately by holding out a pole and saying, "I'm afraid it would be much too long for you." But I say, "No, no, it's perfect," and quickly take it and give him my own broken one. "Thanks. I'll leave it at the rental shop for you," I call out, already skiing away from my bemused benefactor into the swirling snowstorm. His voice barely reaches me, "What's your name? What's your name?"

Two poles of equal length at last. It's so satisfying to concentrate on skiing technically well, rather than just skiing fast. For lack of good health and fitness three months ago, I had to drop out of a race with perfect trail conditions after skiing only 5 kms. Today the conditions are borderline and getting hairier every minute. After 8 or 9 kms I'm monitoring the age-chill factor as well as the windchill, and I'm finding myself amused by both rather than threatened. It's a romp not a race I'm in. I'm suddenly "surprised by joy," the joy of skiing in these conditions.

When the race is over, we gather in Bear Valley's warm yet impressively vaulted lounge for prize giving. Everyone who has taken part gets a prize. C. S. Lewis's story from his book, *Surprised by Joy*, had prompted my own bout of happiness while skiing the last few kilometers. Lewis recounted running cross-country as a schoolboy with one of his masters, a man with much "gusto," when they were caught in a torrential downpour. His teacher's ebullient response to the storm helped Lewis realize that misfortune could be "treated as a joke, a rough joke, a romp." And it *was* a romp for those of us who had gathered to celebrate another spirited skier, Tom Reichle, the race's namesake. ❋

*A Bear Valley warming hut put to good use*

# Area 20—At a Glance

### Yosemite Cross Country Ski Center
Badger Pass Ski Area, CA 95389
phone (209) 372-8444          fax (209) 372-8673
Ski Conditions (209) 372-1000
Weather/Road Conditions (209) 372-1489
Yosemite Reservations (559) 252-4848

### Distance From
Los Angeles—320 mi. South Lake Tahoe (via Sacramento)—316 mi.
Bay Area—214 mi.      Sacramento—172 mi.          Manteca—127 mi.
Fresno—105 mi.        Merced—100 mi.       Yosemite Village—20 mi.
Hwy. 120 (from Manteca), Hwy. 140 (Merced), and Hwy. 41 (Fresno) are the only winter routes to Badger Pass Ski Area.

### Elevation, Facilities, & Hours
Trails—6,500-7,214'   Groomed (skate lane)—17 kms; (track)—40 kms
Marked trails—144 kms    Downhill lifts              Camping
No dogs                  Hours—8:30 A.M.-5 P.M.

### Fees & Rental Prices
Day fee to enter Yosemite National Park $20. No trail pass required.

|                          | Adults/Seniors | Child |
|--------------------------|----------------|-------|
| **All-day skis, boots, & poles** |        |       |
| track                    | $15            | $9    |
| skating                  | $17            | -     |
| **Telemark boots & skis**    | $19        | -     |
| **Snowshoes**            | $11.50         | -     |
| **Sleeping bag**         | $10            | -     |

### Ski School
**Packages:** 2 consecutive 2-hr. lessons with equipment $40; Trail and off-trail tour & lesson (minimum 3 people) $35, with equipment $45; Downhill lesson $20, with equipment $30; Private lesson $26.25; each additional person $16.50.

### Overnight at Glacier Point
Includes lunches (2), dinner, breakfast, lodging, guide, and instruction $110; 3-day tour (when 5 or more sign up) $150 per person; Midweek overnight Glacier Tour with all-day lessons Mon.-Tues. and overnight trip Wed.-Thurs. (includes equipment) $170.

### Ice Skating at Curry Village
20 miles from Badger Pass 7 days per week

|                    | Adults | Child  |
|--------------------|--------|--------|
| **Skate pass**     | $5     | $4.50  |
| **Skate rental**   | $2     | $2     |

For rink times call (209) 372-8341.

# 20 Yosemite National Park

# Badger Pass

## AREA 20. YOSEMITE CROSS COUNTRY SKI CENTER

### Summary

Founded in 1935, Yosemite's Badger Pass is the oldest commercial downhill and cross-country skiing area in California. There are 40 kms of marked trails, of which 17 are on the Glacier Point Road, which leads to one of the most outstanding viewpoints in North America. When it's groomed, this road is a good skating route all the way out to Glacier Point Lodge. You can stay overnight here on a guided tour, or you can ski in and out (as I did) to make a 34-km day trip. Because there's a lot of climbing on this route, you need to be fit to complete it as a day trip. Before making the long drive to Badger Pass, first check that your skating route has been groomed for its entire length. Call (209) 372-8444 and ask to speak with the manager of the cross-country operation.

### Special Warning

Listen to the weather forecast for the Central Sierra before setting off. There's no point in driving here if Badger Pass is inaccessible due to storm conditions or unplowed roads. Typically, when a snowstorm dumps a few feet on your destination, it can take a day or two for area roads to be reopened. **Remember to carry chains—it's the law!**

## How to get there

*From the Bay Area or Sacramento* either drive south to Manteca and turn east off Hwy. 99 onto Hwy. 120, or continue south on 99 to Merced and turn east onto Hwy. 140. *From Los Angeles* drive to Fresno and go north off Hwy. 99 on Hwy. 41. Highways 120, 140, and 41 converge in Yosemite National Park (becoming 120 in Yosemite Valley). If you approach on Highways 120 or 140, go south on Hwy. 41 for 9.5 miles to Chinquapin. Approaching from the south on Hwy. 41, drive directly to Chinquapin. (There's a public bathroom and a telephone here in a small snowplowed lot, opposite a lone house.) From Chinquapin drive 5 miles northeast on the gated Glacier Point Rd. to the large parking lot at Badger Pass Ski Area.

## Description of area

The Badger Pass Downhill Ski Area parking lot serves the cross-country area as well. There are five short lifts and five short ski runs at this small, intermediate downhill operation, and its layout makes for excellent telemark skiing. The groomed cross-country trail, which you've come so far to ski, is the unplowed Glacier Point Road. It's a wide route, groomed specifically for the 17-km (10.5-mile) ski to Glacier Point. Several adjoining unplowed roads can be safely skied and used for overnight camping trips.

*Ranger Bandy points out the route to Glacier Point*

Starting from the flat at Badger Pass, your route to Glacier Point has a few, mildly undulating sections before becoming a long, unbroken 10-km uphill grind. It's not steep though, and there are some nice views east. When the road levels off you're on a ridge, forested at first and then open. Where a meadow slopes slightly downhill on your left you'll find a storm-proof hut. It's a wilderness john.

Staying on the trail, you ski consistently but only slightly downhill until you reach a black-and-yellow road sign, which may be poking out of the snow at trailside. This sign says it all: a black truck on a steep, black downhill slope. This image, tipped a full 35° downward, is a warning to truck drivers (in summer) that they're approaching a dangerously steep hill. And yes, if you're a truck driver or a poor skier, you are!

Steep with many delicious, switchback curves, this section is easy to ski because of the road's wide grooming. Descend through these curves all the way to Glacier Point, where you get the unforgettable view. Both in front of and below you is the panoptic view that many Yosemite veterans insist is the finest in the entire park. If you're staying overnight at the timber lodge here, you'll be able to rise early when the light's best for photography and confirm the view you thought you'd dreamed.

## Where to stay and eat

If you are doing the Glacier Point Overnight Ski Trip, you'll stay in the **Glacier Point Lodge**, an elegantly designed timber building. Lunch on the trail, dinner, breakfast, and another lunch are provided. Your guide will cook for you but you are allowed to help. A one-night trip is $110; a second night at the lodge with day skiing in the area is $150.

The Badger Pass parking lot is 20 miles from one of the most celebrated recreational lodging centers in the world. After driving 5 miles from Badger Pass down to Chinquapin, turn right onto Hwy. 120 and drive 15.5 miles to Camp Curry and Yosemite Village. **Camp Curry** in Yosemite Valley has many types of year-round accommodation including: a canvas tent-cabin for $35, a cabin without bath for $46, a cabin with bath for $69, and a lodge room for $79. If you want a hotel atmosphere, there are two very comfortable ones in Yosemite Village (and a third in Wawona, on the Hwy. 41 approach to Badger Pass).

At **Yosemite Lodge** there are large, comfortable rooms priced from $79 to $96. At the world-famous **Ahwahnee** (the Queen of England has stayed here and she's fussy about where she stays) there are many elegant rooms, parlors (suites), and cottages, ranging from $223 to $269. At **The Wawona Hotel**, the prices range from $82 to $105.

The hotel winter rates quoted were for the '98-'99 season; they do not apply on Thanksgiving, Christmas, or national holidays. All these hotels have excellent dining rooms. Camp Curry has inexpensive, good cafeteria-style meals in an outstanding **Food Pavilion**. In Yosemite Village are a bank, a post office, a medical center, food shops, a church, and a gas station for your convenience. Because you're a long way from other such facilities in the park, check your fuel gauge before leaving.

## *Ninja at Glacier Point*

Snowstorms kept me out of Yosemite each time I'd scheduled to go down there. The second time, at the end of the season, I waited for the storm to abate and drove in on the Wawona route from the south, having arranged with Dave Bengston, the Yosemite cross-country skiing manager, to do the last Glacier Point overnight trip for the season. I got into the park but the pooh-bahs had decided not to plow the 5 miles from Chinquapin to Badger Pass. They simply closed the area a few days early and, at their own convenience a few days later, plowed the road to Badger Pass.

Undaunted by these logistical setbacks, I drove down a third time and put the urgency of my case (author has a deadline by which to write a book covering every Nordic ski area in California with one site, sacred Yosemite, missing) to veteran Ranger Bob Bandy. He met me at Chinquapin, took stock of my request, and let me in. He not only unlocked the gate but escorted me to Badger Pass and saw me off on the trail to Glacier Point.

I knew this day trip was going to be an endurance test—34 kms (21 miles) round trip on a trail that hadn't been groomed for three weeks. With the air temperature in the low 50s, there was bark, lichen, and pollen dust everywhere. My mission was clear: ski in to Glacier Point, take some photos, and ski out. I planned to be in and out in six hours. There would be no other skiers or possible support in an emergency, so I carried a lot of gear, using two small packs. One was up front on my chest with food and fluids; the other on my back was packed with overnight survival in mind—extra clothing, waterproof jacket, ground sheet, and flashlight. While this two-pack technique ensures a balanced load for skiing, I intended to drop one pack strategically along the way.

The first mile was easy. Two snowplows were already clearing the Glacier Point Road for summer tourists, and Bob Bandy had radioed their operators that I was coming through. Luckily for me, the plowers used a technique that removed all the surface snow down to a thin sheet of ice, which had bonded to the tarred road surface. Over this continuous ice sheet my long touring skis (215 cms) glided easily and fast as I simply double-poled up the road.

Now I was on dead snow. Because it has no dry crystals, snow like this damp blotting paper offers a poor glide. Under these conditions the earlier you start the better, but I wasn't early. Under my skis' midsection the crown pattern helped me step into my stride but couldn't compensate for the glide. Since my long skis also failed to improve my glide, wherever the wide undulating trail sloped downward I skated to break the repetition of striding. Often I climbed diagonally up

*Two atheletes training on snowshoes*

snowbanks so that I could telemark down, adding more variety to my skiing.

Four mph is the best I can average on this snow. After two hours' trudging up an interminably long hill I come to an open space, which must be a meadow in summer. There's a building ahead of me. It looks large enough to be a lodge, but sizing objects over open, snow-covered ground can be deceptive. What I reach isn't even a hut, it's a storm-proof john. But with a wind-breaking porch even locked it can be my shelter in the event of a storm. I drop my backpack off here, estimating by my watch there isn't far to go.

The trail continues into forest, and beyond the downhill truck sign I'm soon skiing steeply downhill on parallel skis. What a relief to finally have some glide—playtime after three hours of hard slogging. The snow's softness lets me ski any way I want, following the unplowed road's curves. These conditions are perfect for the jump turns I devised long ago, my "tiptoes."

When I reached the road sign with the runaway truck, I knew my allotted time for skiing in was just about up and I considered turning back. I knew my goal wasn't far away, but I also knew the fast descent would incur a heavy debt repaid only by a steep climb. But thank God (the one who invented snow and lets us play on skis) I did ski down. Snaking downhill through the forest, using the sloping trailside banks for extra gravity, I made many perfectly timed turns and found myself, suddenly, at Yosemite's famous view.

Since I'm skiing solo, I stand my skis in the foreground to take a photo. Below me, Yosemite Valley splits into two, with Tenaya Creek and 8,842-foot Half Dome to the northeast. My eyes are also drawn due east to Merced River waterfalls pouring their 1,000-foot, vertical milklike streams down to the valley floor. I'm standing high above this astonishing world of granite walls and waterfalls when a deep, probing sound penetrates my spellbound concentration.

"Whomp. Whomp-whomp-whomp," comes the deeply resonant sound of some creature whose territory I'm in. When I look where the sound is coming from, it promptly changes location. I look there and the sound's source has moved again, but now I'm on to it. The sound issues from a mysterious ventriloquial bellows of a large, ground-dwelling gamebird that prefers high ground in winter. Though almost tame it's so adept at staying out of sight that it seems to have mastered the ninja art of invisibility. While I swear it's very close to me, the next "whomp-whomp" seems nowhere near. Finding the bird is a losing game; while I can't pinpoint its exact position I do know who this teaser is. It's a blue grouse whose sleight of sound (actually made by pumping an air sac) and ninja skills (ones I've practiced myself for many years) give me much pleasure. ❄

*The unforgettable view from Glacier Point includes the profile of Half Dome*

143

# Tamarack Lodge Resort Cross Country Ski Center

Box 69, Mammoth Lakes, CA 93546
(800) 237-6879    phone (760) 934-2442    fax (760) 934-2281
www.tamaracklodge.com        info@tamaracklodge.com

### Distance From

Los Angeles—328 mi.    San Francisco—273 mi.    Reno—167 mi.
Sacramento—153 mi.

### Nearest Airport

Mammoth Lakes Airport—8 miles
(Non-commercial; commercial by 2001)

### Elevation, Facilities, & Hours

Trails—8,600-9,127'    Groomed—40 kms    Dogs—off groomed trails
Restrooms (2) & cafe (1) on trails    Snowshoeing—off groomed trails
Hours—8:30 A.M.-5 P.M. midweek, 8 A.M.-5 P.M. weekends.

### Passes & Rental Prices (free trail pass for children 10-)

|  | Adult | Jr./Sr. (11-18/65+) | Child (10-) |
|---|---|---|---|
| Trail pass | $16 | $11 | - |
| Skis, boots, & poles | $16 | $16 | $14 |
| Snowshoes | $16 | $16 | $14 |

### Ski School

|  | Adult | Jr./Sr. (11-18/65+) | Child (10-) |
|---|---|---|---|
| Packages (include lesson, equipment, & trail pass (A.M./P.M.)) | $42/$35 | $36/$30 | $25/$20 |
| Lesson with trail pass | $30/$25 | $25/$22 | $12/$12 |
| Group lessons 90-min |  |  |  |
| (A level & B level, learn to skate, downhill, custom ski tours, private) | $15 | $14 | $12 |

### Shuttle

Ride the free Orange Line shuttle to and from Gondola Village in Mammoth Lakes (8 A.M.-5:30 P.M.).

### Lodging & Food

Tamarack Lodge is a year-round destination resort, (800) 237-6879. Winter rates range from $55 for a room (double occupancy) midweek to $270 for cabin sleeping 6-9. Ski Package for two includes trail pass, rentals, lesson, 3 nights lodging $318. Excellent dining room; coffee and snack bar in lounge.

# 21 MAMMOTH LAKES

# ANSEL ADAMS WILDERNESS

## AREA 21. TAMARACK LODGE RESORT
## CROSS COUNTRY SKI CENTER

### Summary

With Mammoth Mountain as its Alpine skiing draw and Mono Lake nearby, Mammoth Lakes rivals Lake Tahoe for skiing and outscores it for scenic wonder. It also has an excellent cross-country skiing area at Tamarack Lodge, just 3 miles southwest of the town of Mammoth Lakes. While it's not big (40 kms groomed), it is the highest Nordic area in California. Most trails are on wide, unplowed roads at elevations varying from 8,600 to over 9,000 feet, resulting in plenty of good, dry snow and a long season. With its broad range of rooms and cabins, pleasant lounge, and excellent dining room, Tamarack Lodge is a comfortably stylish place to return to after a day's skiing. Mountain and lake views throughout the whole area are stunning.

### How to get there

*From Reno (and points north) or Los Angeles (south)*, take the only winter route to Mammoth Lakes—Hwy. 395. At the Mammoth Lakes exit, 164 miles south of Reno, turn west on Hwy. 203 and drive through town to Lake Mary Rd. Follow the sign on your right to Tamarack Lodge. From Mammoth Lakes at 7,900' you have to drive 3 miles uphill to Tamarack Lodge at 8,600'. Although the roads are well plowed, you should carry chains if you're not in a 4WD vehicle. *From San*

*Francisco, Sacramento, or anywhere west of the Sierra*, take Hwy. 50 east to the junction of Hwy. 89 in Meyers (just before South Lake Tahoe). Take 89 (open year-round) south over Luther Pass to the junction of Hwy. 88. Turn left and drive northeast to the junction of Hwy. 395 in Minden. Drive south on Hwy. 395 to Mammoth Lakes as decribed above.

## Description of area

I found that Tamarack Lodge, though offering less groomed-trail mileage than some, to be one of the most pleasant cross-country skiing areas in California. The use of unplowed paved roads as skiing routes ensures wide trails, allowing optimal grooming for set tracks and skating lanes. Where your trail is on a road (not all of them are), the gradients aren't going to be too steep. Already at a higher altitude than other cross-country ski areas, you begin skiing from Tamarack Lodge in an aerobic zone and can climb above 9,000 feet.

Throughout the area, secondary trails branch from main trail arteries and offer more varied and technical routes, which wind through woods and skirt numerous lakes. Lake Mary, Lake George, and Horseshoe Lake stand out as ski destinations from Tamarack Lodge. While Lake Mary Rd., which leads to the entrance of Tamarack Lodge, is unplowed beyond the lodge, it's groomed for skiing 5 kms farther to Horseshoe Lake.

Looking south from here, you face memorial wildernesses named for luminaries such as Ansel Adams and John Muir. Distant Mt. Isaak Walton rises impressively to 12,099 feet. You'll have another fine view from the high ground looking southwest toward Mammoth Crest, where Crystal Crag juts out. Near the lodge there's a remarkable view just off Lake Mary Rd. over Twin Falls down to Twin Lakes. To see it go off the trail a few yards and take off your skis to do so. Over loose snow move slightly downhill onto a little shelf to get your view.

*These Tamarack skiers would agree with the saying, "if you can walk you can ski"*

While this jog can be skied by competent skiers, woe betide you if you can't stop!

At lodge level there's plenty of easy, flat skiing for beginners through forest and around Twin Lakes, with a range of cliffs forming an impressive backdrop. Some intermediate slopes near the lodge are ideal for practicing telemarking and downhill skills. Snowshoers and people with dogs must travel off the skiable portion of the groomed trails; they may use the packed area beside the skiing routes.

Nancy Fiddler, one of North America's most outstanding women skiers, twice an Olympian, 14 times a US Champion, and course record holder for The Great Race from Tahoe City to Truckee, is director of the ski school. Nancy and Barbara Cameron (who was racing at Eagle Mountain) are particularly involved in school programs, inspiring children and coaching junior cross-country racing teams.

## Where to stay and eat

With the Nordic program adjacent to the hotel, **Tamarack Lodge** offers an ideal setting for cross-country skiers. This resort has been operating for 75 years and was recently purchased by Mammoth Mountain. Its new management under Roy Moyer, with Ueli Luthi from Switzerland running the skiing program, does justice to the exhilarating outdoor environment. The dining room is so popular that even in-house guests need to book their table for dinner. (For reservations call (760) 934-3534.) The lobby/lounge has a great fireplace and is quite spacious; a snack and coffee bar is in operation throughout the day. Around the main lodge are many, fully equipped cabins. Depending on the season and the number in your party, your lodging can range from $85 to $290 per day.

Three miles away in Mammoth Lakes are scores of well-known, brand-name hotels among many others. A major Alpine skiing destination, Mammoth Lakes has a huge day- and weekend-skiing population. The room count for rentals is over 8,000. For the many restaurants and hotels in Mammoth Lakes, call the Visitor Bureau at (888) 466-2666. There is an excellent, all-seasons visitor center in Mammoth Lakes on Hwy. 203, on your right soon after you exit Hwy. 395.

## *Marathon Man*

The drive via Mono Lake to Mammoth Lakes is exceptionally beautiful. I never see this volcanic moonscape in its semidesert basin, where I've bird-watched and kayaked for many years, without recalling Mark Twain's uninformed comments about the lake's salinity. Although he greatly admired Mono Lake, Twain was a formidable social commentator but not a man of science; he wrote that no one knows why it's so salty. Mono Lake has a saline ecology that, apart from hosting brine flies and brine shrimp, creates extraordinary columns called tufa towers. It was never more beautiful than when I passed it this winter, surrounded by snow.

Though I reached Tamarack Lodge fairly late in the afternoon after the long drive from the Bay Area, I immediately checked in at the Cross Country Ski Center. Within half an hour of arrival I was on my skis, striding uphill on the Lake

Mary Trail. I needed 10 kms under my skis to get my blood circulating before I could think of resting. Tomorrow (March 28) the 19th Annual Tamarack Lodge Cross-country Ski Race would take place over the classic, 26-mile Marathon distance (the distance Greek messengers ran to Athens with news of the victory over the Persians on the plains of Attica in 490 BC). For the skiers tomorrow the race would be measured in kilometers—42 of them—and it would be a lot cooler than it was for those Greeks.

In the morning the weather was perfect. The air temperature was exactly 32° when the race commenced at 9 A.M. The tracks set for the course were immaculate, with a firm skating lane free of any detritus from the trees. Obviously this would be a skater's race, so I decided to ski it that way myself, even though I'd been on striding skis last night. (That was because the snow was too soft to skate well at the end of a warm day.) Today would be only my second attempt at racing this season; that, plus the high altitude, encouraged me to enter the half-marathon of 21 kms rather than go the full distance. Since the highest ground (over 9,000') would be skied both by the long- and shorter-distance racers, I'd be missing nothing in the way of views.

Off we went; at least off went all competitors but me. I took some photos of the start, gave my camera to a friendly bystander, and then played catch-up on the tracks. I did it so well that by the end of the first 5 kilometers I was second out of six starters in my 55-years-and-over age group. Though one man in this class was well ahead of me, I was steadily distancing myself from the remainder. (Once you're over 50, a 10-year age range in competition is a bit tough; a five-year spread is more equitable.) Conditions were superb—allowing some very fast skating—and would become technically more interesting when we got into the forest cover. Soon I was enjoying myself immensely, skating a series of loops on the high ground, rushing through the forest over up-and-down switchbacks with a few tight corners. Then a lovely flat cruise around Horseshoe Lake offered a little respite.

While the full-distance marathoners would have to repeat much of the course, the half-distance skiers would be directed back to the finish earlier, at a checkpoint. But because my racing bib wasn't bearing the appropriate half-marathon symbol to catch the officials' eyes, I skied on and on until it was obvious that something wasn't right. I was getting too tired. I stopped, exhausted, at a checkpoint to take a drink and

*The Tamarack Lodge Marathon route will lead skiers above 9,000 feet*

check my watch. Because I'd been skiing effectively and as fast as possible for 2 hrs., 5 min., I should have completed my 21 kilometers long ago.

I rested for several minutes and took a long drink before I noticed the people skiing through this checkpoint were a lot younger than I, and all of them were skiing well. I asked someone how far it was to the finish, and the answer unraveled me. "Oh, it's only another 7 kilometers, you're doing well." Now it sunk in that these athletes vigorously racing through this checkpoint were skiing the full marathon—and I was too!

"I've been skiing for over two hours, and my course is supposed to be only 21 km," I told a checkpoint volunteer.

"Oh dear, your bib doesn't show you're doing the half-marathon. You're on the long course; you should have turned off, way back." In my 2 hr.-5 min. time I'd skated 37 kms. But I was too exhausted to enjoy the thought or ski another 7. Fortunately, there was a short route back to the finish line, which I took. All my peers whom I'd outpaced were wondering where I'd been, when I crossed the half-marathon finish last.

The moral of this story is: don't follow Pheidippides, the Marathon Man; he signed up for the whole distance. And, if you don't know where you're going in a race, stick with someone—even if they're slower—who does. I'll chalk this one up as a learning experience. I shall return. ❄

# Area 22—At a Glance

## Montecito Sequoia Cross Country Ski Resort & Winter Sports Center

2225 Grant Rd., Suite 1, Los Altos, CA 94024
Reservations (800) 227-9900
Road conditions to lodge (800) 843-8677
www.montecitosequoia.com    groupsales@montecitosequoia.com

## Distance From

San Francisco—245 mi.    Los Angeles—240 mi.    Fresno—55 mi.

## Nearest Airport

Fresno-Yosemite International—55 miles

## Light Aircraft

Chandler Municipal Airport (West Fresno)—55 miles

## Elevation, Facilities, & Hours

Trails—6,600-7,800'    Groomed—60 kms    Telemark—1 lift
Tours                  Ice skating        Snow play
No dogs                Snowshoeing        Hours—8 A.M.-5 P.M.

## Passes & Rental Prices

|  | Adults | Child (12-) |
|---|---|---|
| Trail pass | $12 | $8 |
| Rentals (1 day/full weekend) | $16/$28 | $10/$15 |

Lodge guests discounted on multi-day rentals.

## Ski School

|  | Adults | Child (12-) |
|---|---|---|
| Learn to ski (day rental, trail pass, & lesson) | $36 | $20 |
| Skier's package (day rental & trail pass) | $26 | $14 |
| Snowshoe rental & trail pass | $20 | $12 |

## Lodging & Food

The Lodge at Montecito Sequoia is a family oriented year-round outdoor-recreation and winter-sports center. Pay for your lodging and meals on (or before) arrival and put your wallet away. 3 meals per day, soups, hot and cold drinks available all day, and comfortable rooms, all for $110 per person per day.

## Alternative Lodging

If you're snowbound at Grant Grove—unable to drive the the road into Sequoia Lodge (the gate is locked)—there's a hotel with cafeteria right by the gate. But before you leave Fresno, when weather requires caution, call the Sequoia Lodge for road conditions. If they're bad, stay overnight in Fresno. Before you turn east onto Hwy. 180, Hwy. 99 has many hotels and restaurants.

# 22  KINGS CANYON NATIONAL PARK
# GRANT GROVE

## AREA 22. MONTECITO SEQUOIA CROSS COUNTRY
## SKI RESORT & WINTER SPORTS CENTER

### Summary

Spacious and remote Sequoia Lodge, in Kings Canyon National Park, is the base for a comprehensive, family winter-sports center. It is situated near Grant Grove, home of the oldest and largest trees on the planet, the giant sequoias. A reliable 4WD or a chain-equipped vehicle is obligatory in this winter wonderland. Pay particular attention to road conditions before approaching Kings Canyon. There is a vehicle escort service for guests between Grant Grove and Sequoia Lodge during bad weather. Call (800) 843-8677.

Montecito Sequoia has 35 kms of well-groomed trails with terrific views over mountain terrain and another 25 kms on lower, flatter terrain. Ice skating, snowshoeing, tubing, and telemarking are all part of the winter program. Indoor activities include Ping-Pong, slide shows, bingo, and other games. A variety of soups, and both hot and cold drinks, are always available in the lodge without extra charge. The rooms are comfortable and the buffet-style meals are well balanced, catering to vegetarians as well as omnivores. Both lodge staff and skiing staff are always accessible and helpful. This is the ideal snow-holiday center for children.

*The winter program caters to every age group for snow play as well as skiing*

## How to get there

*From the Bay Area* take I-580 east to its junction with I-5 and head south on I-5. After 108 miles go east on Hwy. 152, through Los Banos. Where 152 ends at Hwy. 99 (at 150 miles), drive south on 99 to Fresno. At 180 miles drive east through Fresno on Hwy. 180 and continue 55 miles, all the way to Grant Grove in Kings Canyon National Park. (During bad weather phone the lodge from Lodgepole Market Center at Grant Grove; this is where you meet the escort vehicle when necessary from Montecito Sequoia Lodge.) Generals Highway, a narrow, 7-mile gated road, climbs from Grant Grove to Sequoia Lodge. *From Los Angeles* connect with Hwy. 99 north to Fresno. Turn east on Hwy. 180 at Fresno and drive to Grant Grove as described above.

## Special Advice

**If you're not driving a 4WD vehicle, you must carry chains.** Their mandatory use is posted at affected elevations on the highway during and after snowstorms. Failure to comply is foolish; you risk losing control of your vehicle besides being ticketed and fined.

## Description of area

From Grant Grove the drive up Generals Highway to Sequoia Lodge will impress upon you the remoteness of your resort. When you reach the lodge you'll be further impressed with its large size, the view behind it, and the fact that you can ski right off the porch onto the groomed trails. Of its two trail systems, the more extensive one covers the 7,200-7,800' high ground, starting at the ski shop only a few yards from the lodge. Along these trails you'll find 35 kms of mostly intermediate skiing through forest and along open ridges, which offer commanding views from north to southwest.

The **Sunrise Traverse Trail**, which climbs 600 feet from its start at the lodge, is a beauty. Most of the climbing is on one very steep pitch designated one-way only so that no skiers descending collide with those climbing. The climb is well worth the view when you reach the top. To the north you can see Mt. Goddard at 13,368 feet, and looking southeast toward the Great Western Divide you can see Alta and Sawtooth peaks, both well over 11,000 feet. In the distance, Mt. Eisen towers over 12,000 feet.

The forest through which you ski is mixed timber, but predominantly red and white fir. Yet the tallest trees you'll see are sugar pines and then there are Jeffrey pines, too. Many tracks in the snow—often side by side—are made by squirrel and snowshoe hare, mule deer and coyote. At a lower elevation of 6,600 feet, the other trail system offers 25 kms over easy and intermediate terrain with great views of Kings Canyon. This is the **Big Meadows Trail System** that is being further developed. A 600-foot surface lift, gaining 150 feet in elevation, has been added in the teaching area close to the lodge for the '99-'00 season.

## Where to stay

The inviting lodge at **Montecito Sequoia** is your home away from home. With more than 200 beds in comfortable rooms—most with private bathrooms—this is a sizable resort. There are also a number of fully equipped cabins near the lodge. The daily fee per person for full board and lodging is a good deal at $110; it includes ample facilities for indoor recreation, too. The dining room area is huge, with another large recreation room adjacent to it, and the buffet-style meals offer a variety of excellent choices. Vegetarians will not be shorted! Your midday option is a hot lunch in the lodge or a bag lunch on the trail, and there are soups, and hot or cold drinks available all day, at no charge. Your car keys are kept at the desk (you won't be needing them) so that staff can plow the parking lots without having to disturb you. If you're not in search of luxury but have active children—old enough to enjoy a skiing holiday—I can't think of a better resort for you.

If you're prevented from reaching Sequoia Lodge due to local road conditions, **Grant Grove Lodge** has good accommodations, a large restaurant, and a general store, (559) 355-5300. If you hear of a snowstorm in the Kings Canyon Region as you come through the Central Valley, call the lodge road-condition number before you leave Fresno, (800) 843-8677. Fresno has a full range of accommodations—budget to expensive—along Hwy. 99. (I stayed one night this winter at Motel 6 for less than $30, just north of the junction with Hwy. 180.)

## "Heja, heja, friskt humor"

Today I skied with Kevin Murnane, director of the Nordic program here, so that he could show me around the Montecito Sequoia area. For the '99-'00 season Kevin, with his wife Valli, will be running the program at Tahoe Cross Country outside Tahoe City (see Area 10). We set off to ski the Sunrise Traverse Trail because I wanted to check out the yurt on that route, which is used as a warming hut. That it's the steepest trail in the Montecito trail system also intrigued me. In this case what you climb you don't have to ski down, because this trail is so steep and curvy that it's designated a one-way-only uphill route for the general skier's safety. How you come down the other side I'll tell after describing our climb.

After we'd stopped to see the yurt we took on the steep part. It gave us an opportunity to demonstrate, by reading the printout of our ski tracks on the snow, how superior skating is to the traditional striding method. Good skiers can skate even when climbing steeply. For a cross-country skier climbing a steep gradient the bottom gear—to use the bicycling term—is the herringbone technique.

You climb in a series of short steps rather than strides, lifting your knees and stamping your skis into the snow, on their inside edges. Your ski tips are pointed well off to the side while ski tails are pointed inward. In this way your skis move obliquely up the hill. Since the pattern left behind by your two skis looks like the slender bones on a fish's spine, the technique is aptly called "herringboning." Each step taken uphill in this manner is backed up by a solid pole plant behind your rear ski. The pole planted is the one opposite the ski being set down in the snow, and this poling is called "single stick." The tempo of your poling—as it should for all your skiing—sets the tempo for your leg work as you stamp up the hill with short, sharp steps.

If you are fit and a competent skater, you can do a herringbone skate up the hill; it's a matter of strength, timing, and execution. With skis in the same V-pattern as before, instead of planting a ski firmly underfoot to make a platform from which to step off, skate on it with your committed body weight going with it. Rather than lifting dead weight at every step, you are

*Kevin Murnane demonstrates the half-snowplow for slowing down in the groomed tracks*

now gliding uphill with half the leg movements the traditional herringbone requires.

I demonstrated the two sets of track side by side, herringboning the first set, then coming down and skating the second set. The evidence was written in the snow: there were two steps for every one skate. I could see, and thus feel, that skating is twice as efficient. And though skating takes more skill and effort, what it takes is repaid with the smooth feeling of rhythm and glide inherent with this movement. Having agreed that skating is an existential pleasure that improves our lot, Kevin and I continued to climb, with the gradient now at its steepest.

A woman is working her way up the steep hill ahead of us with her herringbone technique. She climbs for a while, takes a break, and continues her steady ascent of the hill. As we come up to her—possibly put off by our more rapid progress—she stops and says, "Oh boy, enough of this! I think it's time to go back down." We stop to chat, giving all three of us a good breather. Kevin points out that the trail's a one-way route for safety reasons, and suggests, "Let's work at it slowly. It's worth the effort because there's a great view once you get to the top and a really friendly downhill ski back to the lodge."

So we move on together, with Kevin taking the lead while I bring up the rear. He skates, but I herringbone in order not to overtake our new partner. Besides, I want to help this skier with her technique. While I can see she's strong, I also see what's sapping her strength. The V of her skis is not wide enough across the fall line to give her good support. She plants each ski firmly but flat, instead of on the inside edge that stamps a ledge into the snow. Each uphill step she makes is precarious, and she's making progress only because of her tiring arm support. She's almost pushing herself uphill with her poles. Since the legs are about five times as strong as the arms—particularly in women other than specially trained athletes—with her legs not doing their job, her arm-and-shoulder work is wearing her out. Only this and her determination keep her from sliding backwards.

She welcomes a bit of coaching when I offer it, and we soon iron out these problems. "Pick your knees up much higher, widen the spread of your skis, and bang the inside edges into the snow. Set the tempo with your poles and plant them firmly behind you to back up your legwork." That's all it takes. She's really willing but just needed some tips. I tell her what my coach in Sweden once said when I was complaining about slipping on a steep hill. "You have to attack the hills—*det er det som susan jore!*" (It's what will get you there!) In a short time all three of us are at the summit of the Sunrise Traverse Trail, taking in the view of Baldy Peak and the ridge beyond Kings Canyon. Now, as Kevin has promised, we get a lovely, long downhill ski the several kilometers back to the lodge. ❅

# Appendix 1.

## Recommended Cross-country Skiing Outfitters near Selected Areas

**BEAR VALLEY: Bear Valley Cross Country**, Box 5120, Bear Valley, CA 95223. This equipment, accessories, and clothing store specializes in Rossignol skis and boots for telemark, backcountry, and in-track skiing. Sales, demos, rentals, and ski preparation, (209) 753-2834.

**MAMMOTH LAKES: Brian's Bicycles and Cross Country Skis**, 3059 PB, Chateau Rd., Mammoth Lakes, CA 93546. A variety of manufacturer's telemark and in-track skis—sales and rentals. Also clothing and accessories, (760) 924-8565.

**SODA SPRINGS: Royal Gorge Summit Station** (see Area 3) has a comprehensive equipment, accessories, and clothing store. Fischer and Salomon specialists. Web site: www.royalgorge.com

**SODA SPRINGS: Sierra Nordic**, 21455 Donner Pass Rd., Soda Springs (at the flashing traffic light as you turn right for Royal Gorge off Donner Pass Rd.). With Atomic Skis exclusively and Salomon boots, this shop specializes in performance in-track equipment (skating, classical, and no-wax striding skis). Ski preparation for high performance is the owner's forte. Sales, demos, and rentals, (530) 426-9165. Web site: www.sierranordic.com

**SHASTA: The Fifth Season**, 300 N. Mt. Shasta Blvd., Mt. Shasta, CA 96067. A comprehensive store with everything needed for cross-country skiing, (530) 926-3606.

**TAHOE CITY: Alpenglow**, 415 North Lake Blvd., Tahoe City, CA 96145. Fischer and Salomon skating and track skis, with ski preparation. Specializing in Karhu skis for backcountry and telemark. Full range of clothing and accessories, (530) 583-6917.

**TRUCKEE: Paco's Truckee Bike & Ski**, 11200-6 Donner Pass Rd., Truckee, CA 96161. Specializing in Fischer and Salomon skis, boots and bindings, and ski preparation for performance. Extensive ski clothing and accessories. Clinics and sponsorship for racing events, (530) 587-5561. For orders call (800) 645-7772.

# Appendix 2.

## A Short Annotated Reading List

Jeneid, Michael, and Tom Martens. *Five Easy Turns—for Cross-Country Skiers.* Stinson Beach, CA: Nordic Ski Press, 1981. For this guide to cross-country ski turns, I did the ski demonstrations and the writing while Tom did the photography and the editing (he was Editor of *Tahoe World* and *Sierra Sun* newspapers when I had a column in both weeklies). This book is obtainable through Nordic Ski Press, Box 1060, Stinson Beach, CA 94970.

Petersen, Paul, John Morton, & Rick Lovett. *The Essential Cross-Country Skier: A Step-by-Step Guide.* Camden, ME: Ragged Mountain, 1998. This comprehensive "how to" covers all aspects of cross-country skiing. The expertise within these covers comes primarily from one of North America's leading ski instructors, Paul Petersen. Paul was on the Professional Ski Instructors of America National Demonstration team for 12 years and is the architect/owner of one of the best cross-country ski areas anywhere. Coauthor Rick Lovett is a full-time writer and avid cross-country skier. Another skiing luminary and Olympic coach, John Caldwell in Vermont (I was coached by him), led the way with his easy-to-follow "Bible of the sport," *Cross-Country Skiing*, published 25 years ago by the Stephen Green Press. Paul reminds me of Caldwell and his book makes a good companion to this one.

Wiesel, Jonathan. *Jonathan Wiesel's Cross-Country Ski Vacations: A Guide to the Best Resorts, Lodges, and Groomed Trails in North America.* Santa Fe, NM: John Muir Publications, 1999. I like this book because it covers a tremendously wide sampling of upscale resorts throughout North America. Jonathan's upbeat and concise descriptions tickle my memory of experiences at many of these areas in Canada and New England.

## A Note on the Author

While teaching experiential education at Boston University in 1972, Michael Jeneid was fully certified by P.S.I.A. He started his first Nordic ski school in the Green Mountains of Vermont in 1975. An international marathon racer who twice won Sweden's coveted *Vasa* Medal, he has skied the *Vasalopp* five times and the 100-mile Canadian marathon, *Coureurs de Bois*, twice. He came to California in 1979 to start the cross-country ski school at Clair Tappaan Lodge in the Sierra. He has been an Outward Bound instructor on three continents, an "Outdoors" contributor to the *San Francisco Chronicle*, and this is his fourth book on cross-country skiing.

# Index

# Read This

Cross-country skiing—even on groomed trails at the resorts—entails unavoidable risk that every skier assumes and must be aware of and respect. The fact that a trail is described in this book is not a representation that it will be safe for you. Trails vary greatly in difficulty and in the degree of conditioning and agility one needs to enjoy them safely. Some routes may have changed or conditions may have deteriorated since the descriptions were written. Also trail conditions can change even from day to day, owing to weather and other factors. A trail that is safe on a clear day or for a highly conditioned, agile, properly equipped skier may be completely unsafe for someone else or unsafe under adverse weather conditions.

You can minimize your risks on the trail by being knowledgeable, prepared and alert. Check with the ski areas as to weather and trail conditions before travelling to them. Just as important, you should always be aware of your own physical limitations and skill levels, choosing appropriate trails. If conditions are dangerous, or if you're not prepared to deal with them safely, choose a different trip! It's better to have wasted a drive than to be the subject of a mountain rescue.

These warnings are not intended to scare you off the trails. However, one element of the beauty, freedom, and excitement of the winter landscape is the presence of risks that do not confront us at home. When you ski you assume those risks. They can be met safely, but only if you exercise your own independent judgement and common sense.